Women at Work

Sarah Harris

Batsford Academic and Educational Ltd London

Typeset by Tek-Art, London SE20
and printed in Hong Kong
for the Publishers Batsford Academic and
Educational Ltd, an imprint
of B T Batsford Ltd,
4 Fitzhardinge Street, London W1H 0AH

ISBN 0 7134 3551 8

ACKNOWLEDGMENT

The Author would like to thank the Senior Administrative Officer, Mrs.B.Gasser and the Librarian, Miss G.Herwig, of Lady Margaret Hall; Carolyn Brown, Editor of Women's Studies Newsletter of the W.E.A; Susan Bullock of the Editorial Board of History Workshop Journal and Dr Madeline Jones for help and advice with the research for the book; Sue Horwitz for compiling the Index; Shirley Dewsnap for typing the manuscript and Nick Harris for patiently correcting the English and many helpful suggestions about the text.

The Author and Publishers would like to thank the following for their kind permission to reproduce copyright illustrations: Birmingham Library, Local Studies, Black Country Workers Collection, fig 19; Birmingham Library, Local Studies, Bourneville Collection, figs 16, 17, 39; BBC Hulton Picture Library, figs 1, 5, 13, 23, 28, 32, 37, 38, 41, 42, 46, 49, 50, 52; The Trustees of the British Museum, fig 4; Camera Press Ltd, fig 59; Henry Grant AIIP, figs 51, 56; GLC Photographic Library, fig 7; The Imperial War Museum, figs 29, 30, 33, 34, 35, 36, 48; Keystone Press Agency Ltd, figs 53, 55, 57, 58; The Labour Party Photographic Library, figs 44, 45; Lady Margaret Hall, figs 24, 25, 26, 27; Leeds Library, fig 9; London Transport Executive, fig 31; The Mansell Collection Ltd, figs 10, 21, 22; National Museum of Wales (William Jones, *Coalface 1900*), fig 8; The Tate Gallery, London, fig 2. Thanks are also expressed to Pat Hodgson for the picture research on this book.

Contents

The
Illustrations

1
Introduction

When Ev'ning does approach we home-
ward hie
And our Domestic Toils incessant ply;
Against your coming home prepare to get
Our work all done, our House in order set,
Bacon and Dumpling in the pot we boil
Our beds we make, our Swine to feed the
while;
Then wait at door to see you coming
Home,
And set the Table out against you come.
Early next morning we on you attend;
Our Children dress and feed, their clothes
we mend:
And in the Field our daily Task renew,
Soon as the rising Sun has dry'd the Dew.
Our Toil and Labour's daily so extreme,
That we have hardly ever Time to dream.

In the newspapers of the past few months you will probably have come across a number of reports and articles about women at work. You may have seen reports of tribunals listening to claims of women arguing that they have been discriminated against at work or unfairly dismissed. You may have seen articles about women who have become engineers or carpenters. Women at work are "newsworthy" today, but working women are not new.

The poem at the beginning of the chapter was not written recently by someone concerned to point out the double responsibility many women carry of housework and full-time paid employment. It was written in 1739 by a washerwoman from Petersfield in Hampshire called Mary Collier. She was incensed by a suggestion, made by a Mr Stephen Duck, that women did not work

1   "What off again? I suppose you're going to see the handsome landlady you were talking about in your sleep last night?" "No, my dear, I'm going to the Club," reads the caption to this cartoon of the early nineteenth century.
▼

very hard, and she set out to show that the work a woman did was equal to, if not greater than, a man's work.

Before the Industrial Revolution began towards the end of the eighteenth century, the large majority of people worked on the land. Women took their share of this work, as well as looking after the home and children. If the family spun or wove cloth in their home, the woman would share in that work too. Judgements about her standing in the community and her excellence as a wife were based on the amount of work she did and the number of children she had. In these two ways she made an important contribution to the wealth of the family.

Women from rich families before the Industrial Revolution were not expected to do manual work, but they had to manage their households which, with lots of dependants, could be very large. Women from rich families were valued for the land they brought to their husbands on marriage.

2   *Haymakers*, painted by George Stubbs in 1785. Men and women working together in the fields would have been a common sight in those days.

One of the most powerful men in the Middle Ages, John of Gaunt (whose son became King Henry IV), owed his wealth, and therefore much of his power, to the vast estates brought to him by his first wife, Blanche. Without that, his family would not have held the position it did. By bringing land to her family, an upper-class woman made a very important contribution to the family wealth.

Throughout the sixteenth and seventeenth centuries changes were taking place in the way work was organized by our society. Work was becoming much more specialized, centred in small workshops rather than in the home. These changes reached their peak in the Industrial Revolution which firmly established the factory

6

system and made things more difficult for women who had to work to contribute to the family's wealth. The removal of work from the home to factories made combining work and bringing up children much more complicated. The idea grew that men should be able to support their wives and families from their own wages and that any money earned by women should be an extra. Women's work began to be associated with low pay.

During the eighteenth century attitudes to women in the growing "middling" classes (small landowners, merchants, bankers and traders) were also changing. Their daughters were being reared for a life of leisure. It was more important for them to acquire "accomplishments", like playing the piano, embroidery and water-colouring, than to learn skills of household management. The idleness of wives and daughters became a family status symbol.

A satirical rhyme on the hopes of farmers and their families sums up this change:

1743
Man, to the Plough
Wife, to the Cow
Girl, to the Yarn
Boy, to the Barn
And your rent will be netted.

1843
Man, Tally Ho
Miss, Piano
Wife, Silk and Satin
Boy, Greek and Latin
And you'll be gazetted.

In Jane Austen's novels you can read lively and often satirical accounts of the lives of elegant young women in the early nineteenth century. The main task facing them and their families was to find eligible husbands of easy means. A pretty face, an adequate dowry, a charm of manner and an

3   Women in George Holloway and Company's clothing factory, using steam-powered sewing machines, 1850s. With the mechanization of work in the Industrial Revolution, women found that they had to go out to work in workshops and factories, instead of working at home. This brought them added difficulties.

amenable disposition were the best qualifications to possess. Too quick an intelligence or too sharp a wit could be a serious handicap. Most of the novels end with the marriage of the heroine, and, in a sense, marriage was the end of a woman's independent existence. Her property became her husband's absolutely, she had no rights of her own; indeed, she became her husband's property. She was living in a *patriarchal* society (one run by men, for men) and the principles of that society were enshrined in laws.

The attitudes towards women in the middle and upper classes reinforced the idea that working-class women should not work outside the home. This helped keep women in low-paid jobs, for to have offered women more money would have threatened the right of the man to provide for and control his family. Indeed, it is possible to argue that the leaders of the reform movements of the mid-nineteenth century, which resulted in the Factory Acts and the Coal Mines Act regulating women's and children's work, were more concerned about preserving the social order than about solving the real problems faced by working-class women.

The bracketing of women and children together in the legislation reinforced the idea that women, like children, were unable to look after themselves and were dependent on others — not adults, in fact. In excluding them from work or reducing their working week, the acts failed to take into account that, although society might like to say that a man should support his wife and children on his wage alone, this was usually far too low and the family depended on wife and children working too.

Some middle- and upper-class people criticized working-class women for not looking after their children properly or for being poor housekeepers. No one asked how they were to do all this and work in a factory for sixteen hours a day for less money than was needed to "keep house" with.

4   This cartoon, published in 1809, reflects the same idea as the satirical rhyme on page 7. Farmer Giles and his wife show off their daughter Betty to their neighbours on her return from school. Women with accomplishments like playing the piano but who did not work were a family status symbol. ▼

5   Jane Austen, 1775-1817. ➤

As the nineteenth century progressed, upper- and middle-class women came more and more to represent the wealth and position of their husbands. Working-class women struggled for a livelihood for themselves and their families in the lowest-paid jobs, in the worst conditions.

But by the end of the century women from all classes were beginning to assert themselves. Some upper- and middle-class women began to demand an end to their idleness; the right to equal educational opportunities and entry to the "male" professions such as medicine and the law. Many working-class women extended their participation in trade unions and began the long struggle for equal pay and equal opportunity at work. This book traces the changes in the lives of women at work that have taken place as a result of these efforts over the past hundred years.

6   A nineteenth-century Scottish coal girl in her working clothes. The Coal Mines Act led to particular hardship in Scotland, in areas where there were no other jobs for women.

7   Middle-class concern at what they saw as "poor housekeeping" among the working class led to the introduction of housewifery classes at evening institutes. This is one at Shoreditch Institute, London, in 1907.

2
Working-Class
Women at Work

During the nineteenth century the vast majority of women in paid employment were working-class women, that is, they and their husbands, brothers, sisters, fathers, mothers, worked with their hands for an employer, and earned a wage. Without that wage they could not live, for they had no other income — no savings, no inherited wealth, no property, and there was no unemployment or sickness benefit.

8   Pit women in South Wales queuing for pay in 1905. As labourers on the surface, they earned less than £30 a year.

▼

The Industrial Revolution had brought about the factory system, where people went to one big building to work, instead of working at home as a family — out in the fields or at their looms in the cottage. The idea of the *family wage* (what the whole family earned from their joint work in the fields and at the loom) was replaced by the idea of the *wage for the family man* (he was supposed to support his family from his earnings). In practice, in the working class, his wage was hardly ever enough to do this, and so his wife (and often his children) had to work too.

But, since a wife was not supposed to be working for a wage to support the family, employers almost always paid her a much lower wage, even if she did the same work. As a result, women became trapped in the lowest-paid jobs, working in the worst conditions.

On top of this, since the wife's role was seen as looking after the home, her husband and children, she had to do all that work as well as her paid job, and she had no modern household aids to help her — no detergents, no hoover or carpet-sweeper.

It was this aspect of their lives that all working-class women shared with each other. The Lancashire cotton workers were the elite of women workers, for they could earn the same wages as men in their industry. The pay-lists, based on the amount of work completed, did not differentiate between men and women. The workers also all belonged to the same trade union, paid equal contributions and received equal benefits. Indeed, in 1896 half the membership of the Lancashire cotton unions were women. But even the female Lancashire cotton workers could not escape the extra burden of running the home and looking after the children.

◄ 9   Women weavers at Glover Brothers' Wortley Mills, Leeds, at the beginning of the twentieth century. Girls and young women made up most of the workforce in the textile industry (cotton and wool), and weavers were their largest skilled grade.

Mrs Bolt was a cotton worker whose typical day was described in an article in *The Englishwoman* in July 1912. Having got up at 5.00 a.m., she laid the fire, cleaned the grate, made the tea and woke her husband. She organized the children and took them to the baby-minder on her way to work, where she arrived, with her husband, at 6.00 a.m. At the end of a ten-hour day in the factory she came home, lit the fire to heat the bath water, collected the children and fetched fish and chips for tea. If it was Friday and pay day, after tea she would go shopping for the week's supplies and pay the rent man, the union man and the death insurance man.

Her next job is to blacklead and polish the grate in the living room, before it gets too hot with the fire. It is nearly half-past seven now and Mr. Bolt, who up to now has been sitting on a chair in the open doorway where it's cool, reading the cricket news, proceeds to wash himself and to change into his "second best" preparatory to spending the evening at the Working Men's Club and Institute.

At last the grate and fire irons are shining enough to satisfy Mrs. Bolt's critical taste and she is glad to leave such a "hot shop" to go upstairs to make the beds. Coming down, she debates to herself the advisability of bathing the children or first swilling the flags. The children both being happily at play outside, she decides on the flags. She decides to do "the front" whilst she is about it . . . finally the doorstep.

Mrs Bolt then baths the children and puts them to bed, and prepares Mr Bolt's supper and the breakfast for the morning. It is not, perhaps, surprising that the magazine account concludes with her falling asleep over her cocoa!

Mrs Bolt's domestic responsibilities could have been reproduced in almost every working-class home. As a cotton worker, she had the advantages of being able to earn a relatively high wage and of being a member of the union, which could, to some extent, help the family if, for some reason, Mrs Bolt could not get to work. For not even the Bolts could have managed without her wages.

By far the large majority of working-class women were much worse off. They were employed in "sweat-shops" and domestic industries (the sweated trades), where the pay and working conditions were appalling. The sweat-shops were small workshops where women were employed in such jobs as making hats, jewel boxes, and saddles, for very low wages. Domestic industries (or outwork) were those where the women worked in their own homes for a "middle-man" who paid them for completed articles such as match boxes.

Fur-pulling was an example of a sweat-shop trade:

It is the business of the fur-puller, broadly speaking, to remove the long, coarse hairs from rabbit skins . . . . On entering the house the air becomes thick with millions of almost impalpable hairs which float in it . . . the window is tightly closed, because such air as can find its way in from the stifling court below would force the hairs into the noses and eyes and lungs of the workers.

The two prematurely aged women . . . are sitting on low stools before a roughly made deal trough, into which they throw the long upper hairs of the skin . . . which is afterwards manufactured into felt hats.

The heaps of skins by their side are dried, but uncleaned and still covered with congealed blood. What do they get from it? They each of them say they can pull a "turn and a half" working twelve

10   A woman earning the "family wage" by doing ►
machining. This picture, drawn by H.H.Flere in 1908, was used in the campaign for Votes for Women, asking the question: "Who is fitter to have the vote — the woman who is the real head of the house, or the drunken husband?"

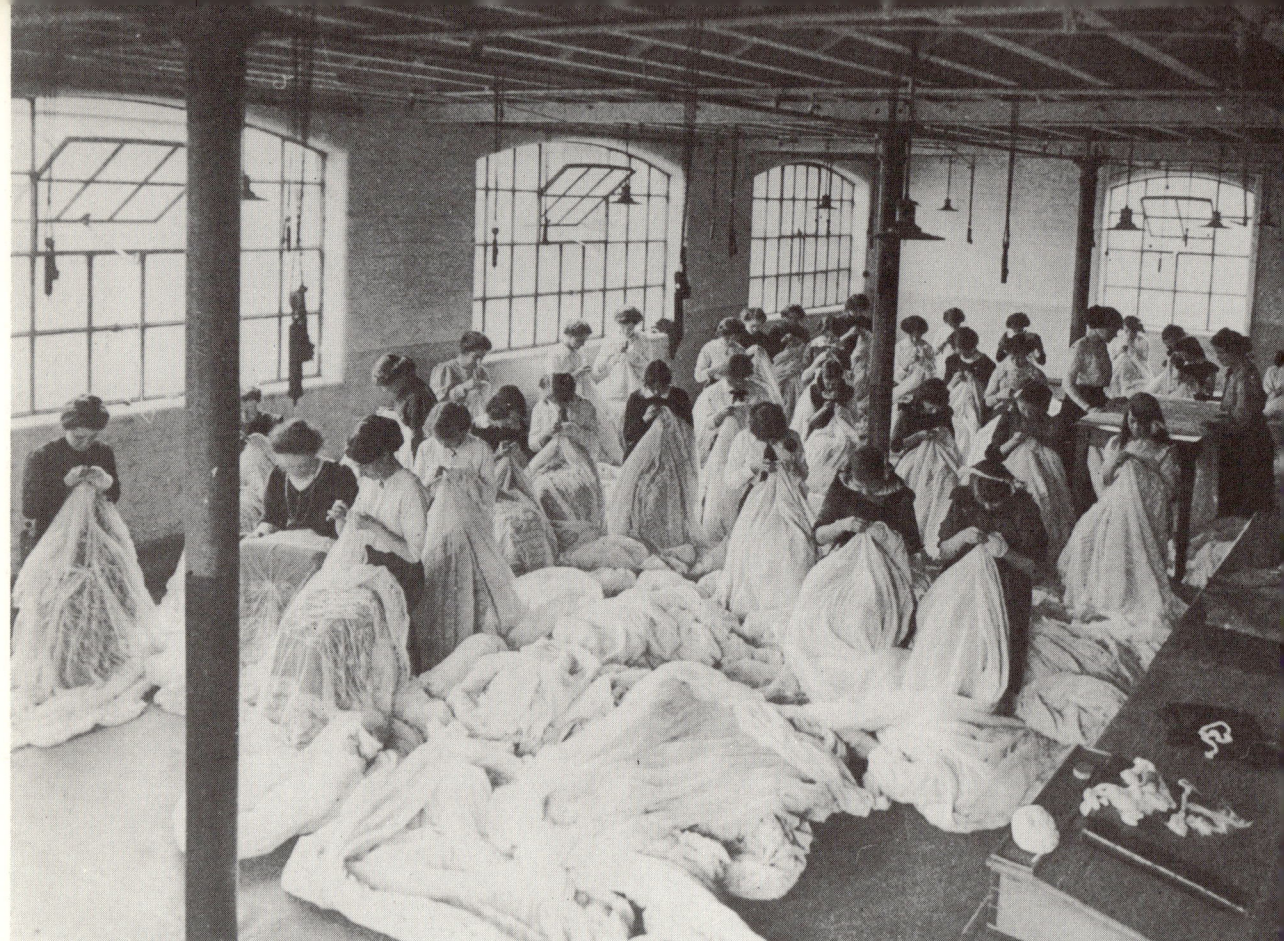

▲
11 Lace makers mending lace broken in manufacture at T.I.Birkin and Company's lace factory in Nottingham in 1914.

hours. A "turn" means sixty skins and the rate of pay is 11d. per turn — 1s.4½d. for the twelve hours. The pulled out hair is carefully selected and weighed at the shop, a turn being supposed to yield two pounds. If the turn is deficient in quantity, the value is, at some factories, deducted from the price of the work.

Other women worked in match factories, jute works, lace factories, iron works, at all manner of tasks. Almost all of them had three things in common: their wages were low, they belonged to no union or benefit society, and they carried the responsibilities of the home. So, even for those women who

were concerned about their pay and conditions, the opportunities to do anything about them were very limited. As one working-class woman, Hannah Mitchell, put it:

No cause can be won between dinner and tea and most of us who were married had to work with one hand tied behind us, so to speak.

Trade unions

Towards the end of the nineteenth century, however, changes were taking place in industry and society which were to have an effect on the lives of working women.

By the 1870s trade unions had been accepted as a permanent part of industrial society. The large majority of them were

16

craft unions, made up of relatively well-paid, skilled men, but the trade boom of the early 1870s (with its consequences of lower unemployment and higher wages) led not only to an increase in membership of these established unions but also to the beginnings of trade unions among unskilled workers, farm labourers and women. The changes taking place in the way businesses were organized helped the growth of trade union membership. The old family firms, whose owners took a fatherly interest in their workers, were being replaced by joint-stock companies, with salaried managers, whom the workers found it easier to stand up to.

Up to 1870 trade union membership among women had lagged well behind that of men. This was partly due to the double responsibility of home and work, the lowly nature of their employment and the resistance of men to women union members.

But from 1870 to 1914 women's union organization increased more than ever before or since.

By 1886, 36,900 women were in trade unions, a 75-per-cent increase in ten years. By 1892 the official estimate was 142,000, and by 1913, 433,000. Though these figures represent only a small proportion of women in work, they were, nevertheless, a significant improvement. The next chapter looks at the way in which these changes came about.

12   One of the earliest demonstrations held entirely by women workers was this one in 1908. A forewoman at the Corruganza box-makers works in southwest London had been sacked for protesting about cuts in pay. The workers went on strike to get her reinstated, and Mary MacArthur and the National Federation of Women Workers supported the strike and organized a march to Trafalgar Square. The forewoman was reinstated.

▼

CORRUGANZA STRIKE TRAFALGAR SQ MEETING

3
Women Unite

Emma Paterson and the Women's Trade Union League

One of the first women to become important in the fight to improve wages and conditions for working-class women was Emma Paterson, who founded the Women's Trade Union League in 1874.

She was born in 1848; her father was a headmaster and she received a good education, including a spell of training to be a bookbinder. When her father died in 1864, she set about earning her own living and was, for a while, assistant secretary of the Working Men's Club and Institute Union. Through this work she made close connections with members of the trade union movement and worked with a woman called Emily Faithfull, trying to form societies of women printers.

In 1873 she married Thomas Paterson, one of the three honorary secretaries of the Working Men's Club and Institute Union. They spent their honeymoon in New York, where Emma Paterson became acquainted with the work of the successful New York women's benefit and trade union societies. She came home determined to do all in her power to help establish successful unions for women workers in England.

She enlisted the help of friends, sympathetic men in the trade union movement, and middle-class philanthropists, and in 1874 the Women's Trade Union League was founded. This was a protective movement, whose object was to persuade women to join or form unions and help remove obstacles that might stand in their way. Trade unions were seen as the best way of improving the wages and conditions of women workers and thus enabling them to clamber out of their "sweated" working conditions. Where possible, the League would finance strikes and stoppages by women workers.

Emma Paterson and those working with her in the League did not accept the prevailing view in society about women workers. They did not think that working was an unfeminine thing to do, and they saw quite clearly that the low wages and bad conditions in which women worked were not really a way of making housework attractive and keeping women in the home, but rather a way of helping the manufacturer make bigger profits by giving him a constant supply of cheap labour. Seeing this as the reason for women's low wages, the League concluded that women should get together or combine in unions, in order best to protect and ultimately to improve pay and conditions.

The League set up a number of societies, including several small unions in London, of bookbinders, upholsterers, shirt and collar makers. Many of these groups were too small

to survive for long, especially since the end
of the 1870s saw a trade recession leading to
cuts in wages and a worsening of conditions
which even the well-established male craft
unions failed to resist entirely.

13 Annie Besant, whose article about the workers
at Bryant and May's match factory helped expose
the appalling conditions there.

Strikes

Towards the end of the 1880s, however, there was a marked rise in the numbers of women deciding to challenge attempts to make them worse off, and even to demand improvements in their pay. Jute workers in Dundee, girls in a tin box factory in London, female cigar workers in Nottingham, and blanket weavers in Heckmondwike came out on strike. The reasons varied, from demands for higher wages to protests against fines imposed for such "crimes" as laughing or singing at work.

The most well-known strike, because it caught the imagination of the public of the day, was that of the match workers at the Bryant & May factory in London. In 1888 an article describing the horrifying conditions under which women worked at the factory appeared in *The Link*, a left-wing magazine edited by Annie Besant, who wrote the article. Called "White Slavery in London", it revealed that adults were earning only 8 — 9 shillings (40-45p) per week and young girls even less — only 4 shillings (20p). It also emphasized the terrible disease caused by phosphorus, called necrosis of the jaw (in which the jaw rotted away), from which many workers in the match industry suffered.

As a result of the article, the women at the factory were asked to sign a document saying that they were well treated. When they refused, one woman was sacked and the rest came out on strike. Uncertain what to do, the women marched to the offices of *The Link* in Fleet Street where Annie Besant agreed to help. With the assistance of the Women's Trade Union League, she and the women established the Match Makers Union, of which Annie Besant acted as secretary. A skilful publicity campaign won a great deal of support for the women, and enough funds were raised to enable them to stay out on strike.

The strike was a success. All the women were reinstated, higher wages were won, the fines were abolished and the Match Makers Union was firmly established. The success of the strike gave a great boost to union organization among other low-paid workers, men as well as women, and a number of new unions were founded, open (unlike the old craft unions) to both men and women.

◄14   The match workers on strike in 1888.

15   A contemporary cartoon, drawing attention to the low pay in sweated trades.
▼

The Trades Union Congress

Women were also taking their place in the Trades Union Congress, the body to which almost all the trades unions belonged. In 1875 Emma Paterson became a delegate to the TUC, representing her union, the Society of Women Bookbinders and Upholsterers. By 1881 there were ten women delegates at the TUC. For women themselves to attend the TUC was very important. By their presence there, they staked a claim for equality with men in union policy making and leadership. The men were by no means sure that they welcomed women in trade union organizations. Henry Broadhurst, a prominent trade union leader, was convinced that factories were unsuitable places for women, who "should be in their proper place, at home".

There was a major difference of policy between many of the women delegates (especially those associated with the Women's Trade Union League) and many of the men, over the question of *protective legislation*. These were the laws which were passed to control the conditions under which women and children were allowed to work. Emma Paterson was particularly opposed to these sorts of laws. She realized that, by continuing to class women with children, they kept alive the idea that women were unable to protect themselves. Such laws also often led to cuts in wages and to the exclusion of women from work at all, as it might be no longer profitable to employ them. Thus women were left much worse off than before.

The men who supported the idea of protective legislation for women did so for a number of reasons. Some believed that women were *not* capable of looking after themselves and therefore needed such laws; others saw the laws as a way of indirectly influencing men's conditions at work, by setting new standards or by forcing factories to cut the working day for everyone.

Emma Paterson and her supporters lost the fight in the TUC, which continued campaigning for laws to protect women's hours and conditions of work. As a result, the League and its members, making the best of a bad job, began to campaign for the appointment of women factory inspectors who might, at least, see that the laws were enforced.

The first woman factory inspector, May Abraham, was appointed in 1893. The reports submitted by her and her colleagues over the following years did much to expose the conditions under which women worked and how dependent they were on the wages they could earn. The Factories and Workshops Report for 1902 contains the following note from Miss Deane:

I find that injury to a finger is regarded as a very slight matter by those unthinking persons who fail to realise how terribly dependent working girls are on these members for their livelihood. The quickness and precision or the delicacy of touch on which so many hundreds depend is destroyed even by a stiff joint, or a maimed or enfeebled muscle; and though indomitable will and much practice may enable a girl to carry on her work under the altered conditions, it is at a lower wage. In addition there are the weary weeks and months of enforced 'out of work', for which the compensation (even if allowed, which is by no means always the case with women and girl workers) is generally totally inadequate. The sum of £20 cannot be held to compensate a working girl for the amputation of her right hand.

I was not surprised therefore when a

16 and 17   These photographs show the canteens, ➤ one for women, one for clerks, at Cadbury's Bourneville factory, in about 1900. The welfare provisions at this factory were better than in most, but there was to be no mixing of the sexes. Note that the male clerks have table-cloths and napkins and are waited on by women.

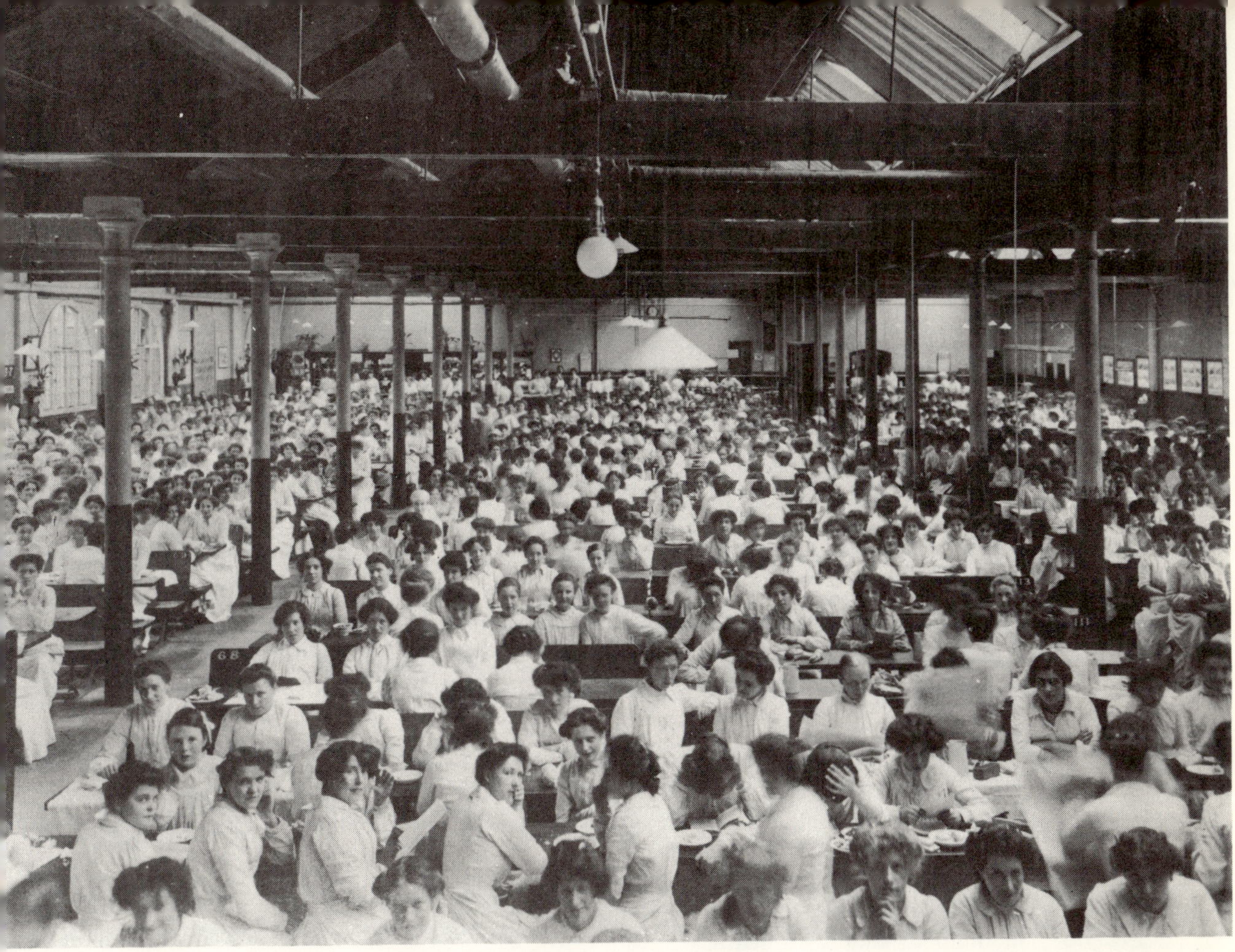

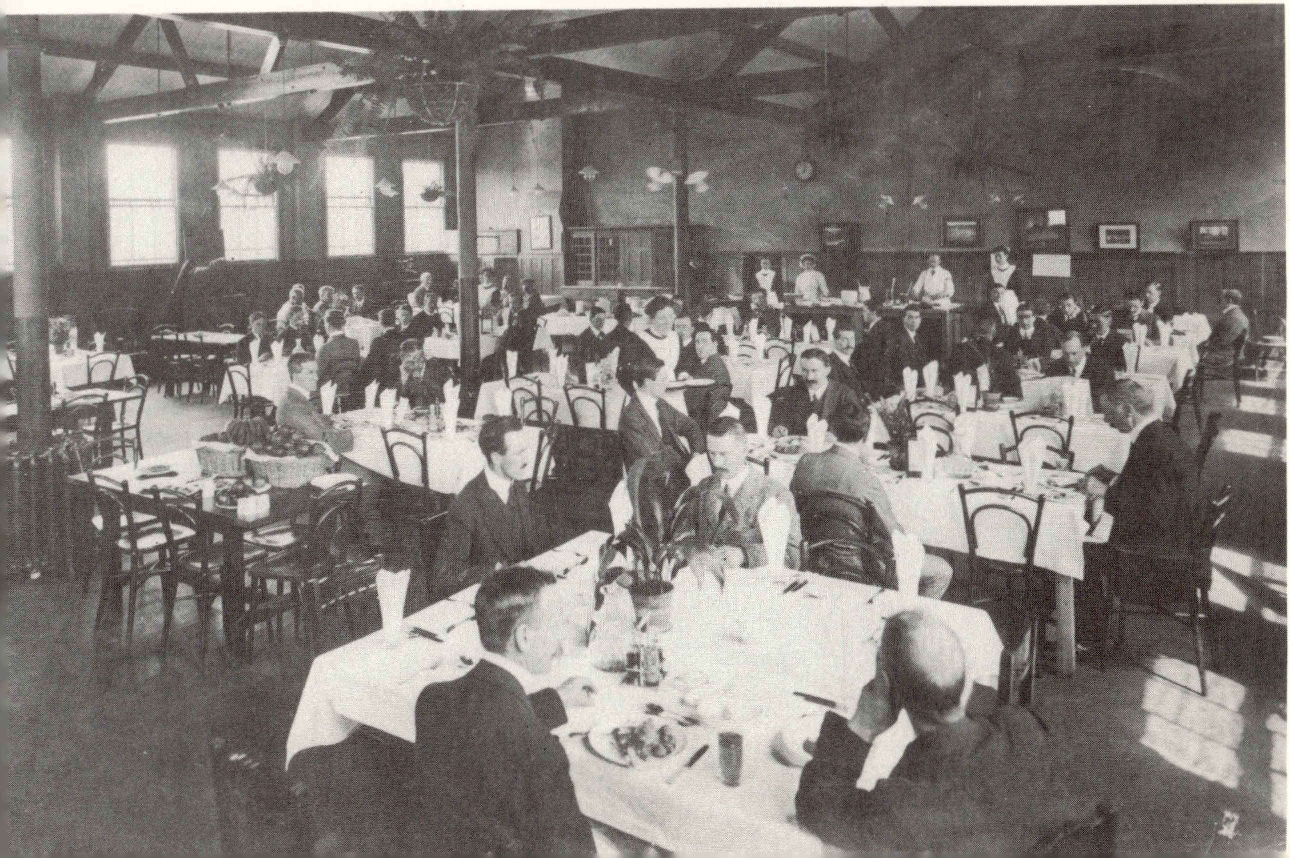

girl explained to me that the loss of her whole foot would have seemed a less serious blow than the loss of her two first fingers for 'I could ha' come to work in a bus with a crutch, but now I can't do my work at all'.

Mary MacArthur

In the new century another major figure in the women's trade union movement emerged. Her name was Mary MacArthur. She was born in 1880 in Glasgow and worked as an assistant in her father's draper's shop. In 1901 she joined the Shop Assistants' Union and the following year was elected president of her union's Scottish District Council. In 1903 she was appointed secretary of the Women's Trade Union League and from then on devoted herself to the cause of bringing women into trade union membership. Returning to the idea of a national general union of women workers, she founded, in 1906, the National Federation of Women Workers by bringing together many of the small, often unstable societies which the League had helped establish. Unlike the League, whose role was to encourage women to join unions but was not a union itself, the NFWW was an organization which women could join and which performed all the functions of a trade union. By 1909 it had 4,000 members.

Mary MacArthur was also deeply concerned about the conditions of women in the sweated trades, most of whom were still working in the conditions which had prevailed fifty or more years before. In 1906 the average male wage was 30 shillings (£1.50) per week; but even women who belonged to the unions in the textile works got only 18s 8d (93p). For women carding hooks and eyes at home, the average wage was only 5s (25p) for 100 hours work per week.

The difficulties of organizing these women into unions seemed almost insup-

erable, and Mary MacArthur supported the idea of protective legislation for such workers. With the help of A.G.Gardiner, editor of the *Daily News*, she organized an exhibition of Sweated Trades. Forty-five trades were represented, from beading shoes to making saddles. The Edwardian public, for whose luxuries the women slaved away, were astonished to discover that the going rate for match boxes was 2¼d (under 1p) for 144 (find your own paste) and 5d (2p) for a skirt.

The Trade Boards Act

As a result of the exhibition, an Anti-Sweating League was formed, the Board of Trade began an enquiry, and the House of Commons set up a select committee. Their combined activities led to the passing of the Trade Boards Act in 1910.

The act set up wages boards representing employers, workers and the government, whose job it was to set a minimum wage in industries where union organization was too weak to be effective. The first trades to be covered were chain making, lace making, paper box making and tailoring. In 1913 six more trades were covered and the act was extended to cover many more in 1918.

But, as Emma Paterson had understood thirty years before, laws on their own were not enough. The act included a clause which gave employers six months' notice of an agreed wage rise. If, in that time, employers could get the workers to agree to work at the old rates, the wage increase would be delayed for another six months and so on, indefinitely.

When, in August 1910, the Chain Making Board published new rates of pay for the industry (increasing them from 4—7s (20—35p) per week to 11s 3d (56½), it became clear that the employers were determined to do everything they could to get the workers to continue at the old wage.

18 Mary MacArthur at the Trades Union ▶ Congress, held in Nottingham, 1908.

24

The NFWW and the Birmingham Trades Council instructed the chain makers not to sign on at the old rates. The employers retaliated by locking them out till early October.

One of the women most closely involved in organizing and supporting the chain makers was Julia Varley, the Birmingham organizer for the NFWW. Unlike Emma Paterson and Mary MacArthur, both of whom were middle-class women, Julia Varley was from the working class. She had started work in a woollen factory at the age of twelve, and at thirteen was on the executive of her union. The following year she was elected to Bradford Trades Council where she served for seven years until 1908, when she joined the staff of the NFWW.

With her organizing abilities and the support of other trade unionists, the chain makers were successful and in October 1910 the new wage rates were accepted by the employers. This victory not only meant that recommendations from other trade boards were now more likely to be accepted, but also resulted in a huge rise in trade union membership among workers in the sweated industries.

However, it remained generally true that, as Mary MacArthur put it:

Women are unorganised because they are badly paid and poorly paid because they are unorganised.

Despite the great strides forward which women workers had made in the forty years up to the outbreak of the First World War, their wages and working conditions were still well below the standards achieved by men.

19   A woman chain maker at Cradley Heath, Birmingham, c.1900, keeping an eye on her child while she works.

▼

4
Girl – Greek and Latin

The demand for equal education

During the second half of the nineteenth century, while working-class women, with the support of sympathetic men and radical middle-class women, were getting together to improve their wages and working conditions, middle-class women themselves were developing ways of putting an end to their purely decorative role. They were demanding equal educational opportunities with their brothers.

The sons of middle- and upper-class families were sent away to school, if possible, preferably to one of the nine public schools such as Eton or Winchester. Here they would learn Greek and Latin and a few other subjects and they would eventually enter Oxford or Cambridge and take a degree. This would qualify them for one of the professions (such as the law or the church) or entry into the government civil service.

The vast majority of upper- and middle-class girls, on the other hand, were educated at home, by poorly paid and often much-despised governesses. Apart from reading and writing, they were expected to master a little French and Italian, play the piano, sing, paint and draw. These were all "accomplishments" which enhanced a young lady's chance of marriage.

A number of women, especially those from more enlightened homes, who had received encouragement to read widely and study further, were profoundly dissatisfied with this state of affairs. Two of the most famous early campaigners for better education for girls were Frances Buss and Dorothea Beale. They were closely associated with the first girls' public day school — North London Collegiate School — founded in 1850, and with the first girls' public boarding school — Cheltenham Ladies' College — founded in 1854. Another pioneer in women's education was Emily Davies who opened a hall for women in Cambridge (Girton) in 1869. These women were campaigners for equal rights, forerunners of the suffragettes who were to demand the vote for women. But the acceptance of the idea of the desirability of better and more education for women and girls was not confined to those who were consciously concerned about women's rights. Many who supported the moves for wider educational provision were indifferent to women's rights as such, and saw education as something to be enjoyed in itself — not a means to an end, but a pleasurable pursuit and one which should be shared by men and women.

One such person was Elizabeth Wordsworth, the first Lady Principal of Lady Margaret Hall, founded in 1879 — the first of the Oxford women's colleges. She wished to give women the chance to share intellectual

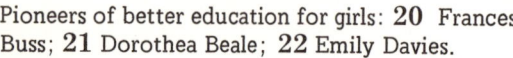

Pioneers of better education for girls: **20** Frances Buss; **21** Dorothea Beale; **22** Emily Davies.

pursuits and pleasures with men. Having no need herself to use her good education to earn a living, she rather despised this view of its purpose.

She was the daughter of the Bishop of Lincoln and great-niece of the poet William Wordsworth. Her grandfather had been Master of Trinity College, Cambridge and her brother was a fellow at Oxford. Added to this impeccable background was the fact that Elizabeth Wordsworth was one of the few lucky women whose parents had encouraged her to pursue her intellectual interests, and so she was widely read and had learned Greek and Latin. When a group of Oxford men and women were looking for a principal for the women's hall which they were determined to open, Elizabeth Wordsworth seemed an obvious choice — not least because of her popularity as a dinner guest where her conversation was regarded as witty and intelligent.

Women at Oxford

The idea that there should be facilities at Oxford for women to acquire a higher education had been mooted early in the 1870s. A change of rule to allow fellows to marry had brought to Oxford a group of young intellectual women who had set about organizing series of lectures for themselves and other interested women in the town. They were given an old room by the University, and sat an exam at the end of each course. Women teachers were admitted free or at a reduced rate. It is interesting to note that the same people who organized the lectures were responsible for starting a trade union among women in Oxford, under the auspices of the Women's Trade Union League.

The lectures were so successful that in 1875 Thorold Rogers, the Professor of Political Economy, proposed that the University should start examinations for women. These were to be different from those taken by men because of the different educational background of the women. There was to be no limit to the time the women could study before taking the exams. They were not required to live for a fixed number of terms in an Oxford College and they could take modern languages instead of Greek and Latin. The Oxford Delegacy, responsible for all the University's examinations, successfully established the women's exams, and the Bodleian Library allowed women to use its reading rooms in the Radcliffe Camera.

23   Women's admission to higher education did not go unopposed. This is a demonstration at Cambridge in 1897 against women in the University.
▼

24 The old building of Lady Margaret Hall, c.1890.

It then seemed sensible to talk about opening a house or hall of residence in Oxford for women who wished to take advantage of these new opportunities. Many felt that if women were to prepare properly for the examinations, they needed to have access to the lectures, teachers and books available in Oxford.

In June 1878 the Association for Higher Education of Women in Oxford was founded. This committee was to be entirely responsible for organizing the lectures, courses and exams for the women. There were to be two halls where women who came from outside Oxford could stay. One would be a Church of England establishment (Lady Margaret Hall), the other non-denominational (Somerville Hall). Those who lived in Oxford could join the Society of Home Students (this later became St Anne's College).

The circular despatched to various people, seeking their support and interest for Lady Margaret Hall, justified its establishment in the following terms:

The precedents at Cambridge and Dublin render it highly probable that the numbers availing themselves of such education will be large, and that a considerable influence will then be exercised directly on the character and culture of English women and indirectly (through teachers and others trained under the system) upon the life of English families and schools.

The founders saw themselves as setting up an institution which would have a wide influence on English life, both by educating the mothers of future generations and by educating the teachers. But it was also perfectly clear that the hall was for women

30

25   A group of the first students of Lady Margaret Hall, with Elizabeth Wordsworth (in white cap).

from middle- and upper-class families. There was no notion yet that working-class women (or men) should go to Oxford.

The first students entered Lady Margaret Hall in October 1879. The Annual Report for 1879-80 commented:

The classes from which the hall has been recruited are mainly those of country gentlemen, clergy and professional men.

There were nine students in all, among them Edith Argles. She was twenty-six years old and the daughter of the Dean of Peterborough. She had been encouraged to enrol by a friend of Elizabeth Wordsworth's, on the grounds that it was important that "women of formed character and principle" were there at the beginning, to set the tone.

Another student, also the daughter of a clergyman, was Winifred Cobb, aged eighteen, who was one of the few students not to have been educated at home. She had been to Cheltenham Ladies' College. Another student, Evelyn Anstruther, was the daughter of a Scottish baronet and a fourth, Edith Pearson, who held a scholarship, was a daughter of a Fellow of the Royal Society, Sir Edwin Pearson.

The life of the hall was designed not only to encourage work but also to ensure that the students continued to develop and behave in a way suitable for young ladies. In the morning they worked together, to save heating costs, and in the afternoon they were expected to take some exercise, such as going for a walk. At tea-time Elizabeth Wordsworth would often have invited her distinguished Oxford friends, and the students were expected to entertain them and so develop the art of good conversation.

31

In the evening everyone gathered in the drawing-room while a book was read aloud and the students tore strips of paper to stuff pillows for the poor.

Wherever they went — to lectures, classes, on walks — they were accompanied by an older woman. They were always required to wear gloves and hats — the latter even when taking a turn around the garden. They were, after all, young ladies, even if they were also intellectual, religious and slightly old-fashioned!

Oxford women at work

To a large extent, the students who passed through Lady Margaret Hall, fulfilled the hopes of the founders. Of twenty-three ex-students mentioned in the Annual Report of 1888-89 all but two were teaching. Of the two who were not, one was a librarian and the other was working for Octavia Hill, a famous Victorian philanthropist, who had set up housing schemes for poor workers in London. Very few of the old students had married.

By the outbreak of the First World War those women who had been to Lady Margaret Hall were to be found in a much greater variety of occupations. This was partly due to the extension of employment opportunities for women since the Hall had been founded, but was also a consequence of the higher educational standards that women were now able to achieve.

About a quarter of the ex-students had married and many of these were engaged in voluntary "good works" such as being Justices of the Peace, or elected members of County Councils. Of the remainder, the majority were school-teachers, but professional social workers (a very new occupation) were beginning to run them a close second. The Civil Service was also a large employer of ex-students, especially at the Board of Trade, and a number of old students were among the first women factory inspectors. Quite a few had become missionaries or entered religious orders — a reflection of the Hall's Anglican foundation. Some became doctors, one of whom, Rosalie Johnson, was among the first women doctors serving in France during the First World War. The Workers' Educational Association found several of its organizers from old students and a number of others were actively involved in the suffragette movement. Miss Royden and Ida O'Malley were successive editors of *The Common Cause*, the newspaper of the National Union of Women's Suffrage Societies.

Perhaps the two most famous ex-students of Lady Margaret Hall from the pre-war era were Janet Hogarth and Gertrude Bell. The career of the former can be seen in some ways to exemplify the opportunities in administration and public service which opened up for determined middle-class women at that time, and it is, to some extent, a model that subsequent generations of educated young women have followed.

Janet Hogarth was the daughter of a

26   Janet Hogarth.

clergyman. She entered Lady Margaret Hall in 1885, at the age of nineteen, and in her final examinations gained a first-class pass in Philosophy. After a few years in teaching, she became Chief Clerk to the Royal Commission on Labour and then, in 1894, went to the Bank of England. She became deputy editor of the magazine *Fortnightly Review* and in 1911 married its editor, W.L. Courtney. During the war she became Adviser on Staff Welfare at the Ministry of Munitions and was awarded the OBE. She also published a number of books.

The career of Gertrude Bell, while hardly being typical even by today's standards, is another example of the opportunities that had come to exist for any woman with enough willpower, education and money. Few men could have matched her achievements.

The daughter of a Yorkshire baronet, she

studied History at Lady Margaret Hall at the same time as Janet Hogarth, and also got a first class in her exams. She was a dynamic and daring young woman, and made her name before the war by her adventures in the Middle East. She was both an explorer and an archaeologist and travelled all over Arabia, visiting and mapping places where no other European had been. She wrote a number of books about her travels, became fluent in several Middle Eastern languages and was awarded the Gold Medal of the Royal Geographical Society. During the war, her unique knowledge of the area led to her appointment to the Intelligence Department in Cairo and in 1916 she was attached to the staff of the Chief Political Officer in Basrah. She was mentioned in despatches for her work four times.

Work or marriage

This was a signal achievement. But for a young woman to succeed in any career at all required a great deal of single-mindedness. Though it was true that, for the vast majority of middle-class women, opportunities had been extended, the conviction that a woman's place was in the home had not been seriously shaken. Most women had to choose between work and marriage. Only a few managed to combine the two, and even fewer were able to combine work, marriage and children. Many employers would not take on a woman who was married, and some operated a marriage bar where women employees who then married were forced to leave their jobs.

So, while the majority of working-class women had to find paid employment in order to make ends meet, as well as cope with home and children, many middle-class women, whose jobs offered more interest, variety and better pay, were forced to choose between their jobs and the opportunity to have a husband and children. In neither class did real freedom of choice exist for women.

27   Gertrude Bell.

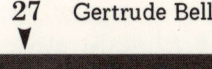

Miss Bell
Orientalist & Novelist.

5
War Work

On the eve of the First World War, of the fifteen million women in Britain five and a half million were in paid employment, of which one and a half million were domestic servants. Between 1914 and 1918 the total number of women in employment increased to seven million, three million of whom were employed in industry, a far larger number than before the war. Many were employed doing jobs which were previously the preserve of men. The wartime increase in numbers and change in the types of work done by women raised questions and challenged attitudes in a way that the more steady changes of peacetime could not have done.

The increase in women's employment did not take place overnight. The initial effect of the war was, rather, to increase unemployment among women. The industries where the bulk of women worked — the cotton industry and the peacetime clothing industry — were badly affected by the outbreak of war, as imports fell and people bought fewer clothes. By September 1914 female employment in these industries had fallen by fourteen per cent.

Some relief work was organized by middle-class women for those women who were unemployed as a result of the war, particularly among the workers in sweated trades, but throughout 1914 and the first half of 1915 there were no fundamental changes in attitude to women and women's work.

Everyone was convinced that war was a man's business — he did the fighting — and that the way of life at home should be as unaffected as possible. The first slogan of the war was "Business as Usual".

Changes were taking place, however. The war required organizing and this resulted in the growth of clerical and administrative jobs which were largely filled by women. To a great extent, this merely confirmed a trend that had existed before the war, for the introduction of the typewriter had already turned secretarial work and clerking into a mechanical task considered suitable for women to undertake. A number of upper- and middle-class women too, caught up in the patriotic feelings which swept the country in August 1914, were anxious to volunteer their services, and a number of voluntary, uniformed groups — such as the first women police patrols — were set up, run by forceful upper-class women and sanctioned by the government. However, it was not until the government confronted two crises in the running of the war that the whole question of women's work was brought under review.

The first crisis was the shell shortage on the Western Front, which led to the setting

28   An Edwardian maid in her uniform. During ►
the war many women were to leave domestic service
to undertake other more diverse jobs.

29 Women police patrol advising a woman traveller at Euston Station, London, during the war.

enlisted the support of Mrs Pankhurst, who had led the militant suffragette movement before the war. With the aid of a grant of £2,000 from the Ministry of Munitions, she and her daughter Christabel led a march of women through Whitehall, demanding "Women's Right to Serve". The march was greeted with enthusiasm, even by such established institutions as *The Times*.

The second crisis was the shortage of men, caused by the massive casualties in France. The need for more soldiers at the Front was becoming so acute that in August 1915 all persons, male or female, were required to register details of their age and occupation. This national registration scheme was the first step in the introduction of compulsory military service for men — or conscription — which was completed in May 1916. If men were to be directed into the armed forces, their places at work would have to be filled — and filled by women. At a meeting in Swansea in 1915 Lloyd George declaimed:

without women victory will tarry, and the victory which tarries means a victory whose footprints are footprints of blood.

Women in munitions factories

In July 1914 212,000 women were employed in those industries which were to become most closely associated with war production — the engineering and metal trades. The numbers for July 1915 (256,000) show a small increase, but by July 1916 — after the Ministry of Munitions had begun positively to encourage women into the work and after conscription had been introduced — the numbers had almost doubled to 520,000. By the end of the war more than 920,000 women were employed in this sort of work, and the increases in these industries accounted for almost the whole of the increase of women employed in all industrial

up of the Ministry of Munitions in May 1915. Lloyd George, who was appointed Minister of Munitions, was determined to increase the production of shells and ammunition. He recognized that, in order to do this, he would need to employ women in large numbers — many of them in skilled and semi-skilled engineering jobs in dangerous workshops, previously the preserve of men. He began a propaganda campaign to bring women into the munitions industry and

30 Women munitions workers during the war. ➤

production between 1914 and 1918.

Many of the women came into this work from domestic service and, for them, it represented a new and previously unhoped-for personal freedom. Rosina Whyatt, who became a trade union organizer after the war, went to work in a munitions factory in Luton and described her own experiences in an account of "Jenny's" life:

Jenny had to clock in at the factory at eight o'clock in the morning. This was new to her and it was a comforting thought that she would not have to get up at five or six o'clock as she had done during her domestic service days. She would start work at 8.00 a.m. and finish at 8.00 p.m. What would she find in this great new venture? She had already a feeling of a new freedom and of time to think.

She was issued with an overall, cap and rubber shoes and set to work making detonators. Dinner was between 1.00 and 2.00 p.m. and consisted of meat, a vegetable and a pudding costing 9d (4p), with tea or coffee 1d (½p) extra. Her wages were 30s (£1.50) for a seventy-two-hour week and every week she paid her 2½d (1p) subscription to the Workers' Union which she joined soon after starting work at the factory.

After a while making detonators, she was moved to a new part of the works:

The next move was the spinning room for an operation to test the springs of the fuses — a very exacting job, requiring good eyesight and constant vigilance to ensure the accuracy of the spring. Without this the fuse would be useless. This operation caused dust and chemicals to fly about the room making the skin and clothes yellow. Jenny had often noticed this among the girls and wondered how they became yellow, they were in fact called "Chaul End Canaries"...
...Not only did Jenny become yellow.

She found after a time that the powder was affecting her skin. Her face, neck and legs began to swell, so much so that she could not see and had to be led home. She was ordered to stay home for ten days on half pay. For three days she could not see anything. On being examined by the works doctor, T.N.T. poisoning was diagnosed. This was something Jenny had not bargained for. She had to be bandaged as the skin had now broken and fluid was escaping; she looked something like a member of the Ku Klux Klan or an Egyptian mummy for some time. But it was a good thing that the fluid did escape, had it gone into the body she would not have lived to tell the tale.

It was weeks before she could dispense with the bandages on her neck and hands, in fact, the effects of the poisoning lasted for months — despite the fact that she had two pints of milk every day to drink.

Poisoning from T.N.T. — the high explosive — was recognized as a major hazard in munitions works. Two women doctors described the range of symptoms in an article in *The Lancet* in August 1916. They included sore chests, coughing, rashes, jaundice, disorders of sight, coma and convulsions. The milk Jenny received was provided free for T.N.T. workers. Protective clothing was also issued, though the sorts of things provided (masks, rubber gloves, and worst of all goggles) made working on the precise tasks impossible. Inadequate though these provisions were, they indicated a slightly improved attitude to safety at work and, thanks partly to the increase of middle-class women employed in the factories, facilities for dealing with sickness and injury were appearing, as well as canteens and toilets for women.

But the war as a whole was conducted against a background of disregard for human life and this was reflected in industry. Workers were expected to work long shifts, overtime was often compulsory. In Leeds a sixteen-year-old hurt her arm in her machine at 7.30 a.m. one Saturday morning. She had been on shift since 6.00 a.m. on the Friday, with only two and half hours away from her machine in that whole time. Her case for compensation was dismissed on the grounds that "the most important thing in the world today is that ammunition shall be made".

Other civilian jobs for women

Munitions was not the only area in which women's employment expanded. The largest proportional increase was in transport,

31　Transport workers: the first tram conductress in London, 1915...

▼

▲
32   ... and women porters at Marylebone Station, London, 1915.

where the number of women went up from 18,000 in 1914 to 117,000 in 1918. This was partly due to the fact that the male transport workers raised no objections to women driving motor vehicles, as this had not yet been established as a "masculine" skill. Many upper-class women became drivers. There was, however, considerable opposition to women driving tram cars — a male preserve — but horse-drawn vehicles could be driven by women, who were supposed to have a particular affinity with animals!

Four hundred thousand women left domestic service for various jobs. One young woman, Winifred Griffiths, found the war gave her the opportunity she was looking for to leave her job as a housemaid. Her commitment to socialist ideas had made her feel very uncomfortable in domestic service:

It seemed very important to me that I should bring my own life as far as possible into line with this ideal. I suddenly saw my present occupation as a useless one — doing things for people that they could quite well do for themselves and helping them to sustain a standard of life completely unjustified while so much poverty existed . . .

. . . the war was changing people's lives. There was a great deal of talk about 'jobs of national importance' for women as well as men. One day Mrs. Scott . . . told me that the manager of the Co-Operative Stores in Basingstoke was on the lookout for young women to train to take the places of grocery assistants who were joining the forces . . . in due course [I] was taken on in the grocery department . . . . I went into lodgings in town where I shared a room and bed with another girl paying 12s 6d. a week for board and lodging. My mother did my washing, for which I gave her 1s. per week. My wage was £1.00 so I was left with 6s.6d. to cover everything else, including running my bicycle.

Besides releasing men from civilian occupations, women were also needed to release men in the armed services from non-fighting jobs, so that the gaps at the front line caused by the huge casualties could be more easily filled. This led to the establishment of women's sections in the forces – the WAAC and the WRNS.

The WAAC (Women's Auxiliary Army Corps) was formally constituted in July 1917 under a Chief Controller, Mrs Chalmers Watson. Instead of officers, there were

33 and 34   Recruitment posters for the WAAC and WRNS, who needed women for non-fighting military jobs in the First World War.

▼

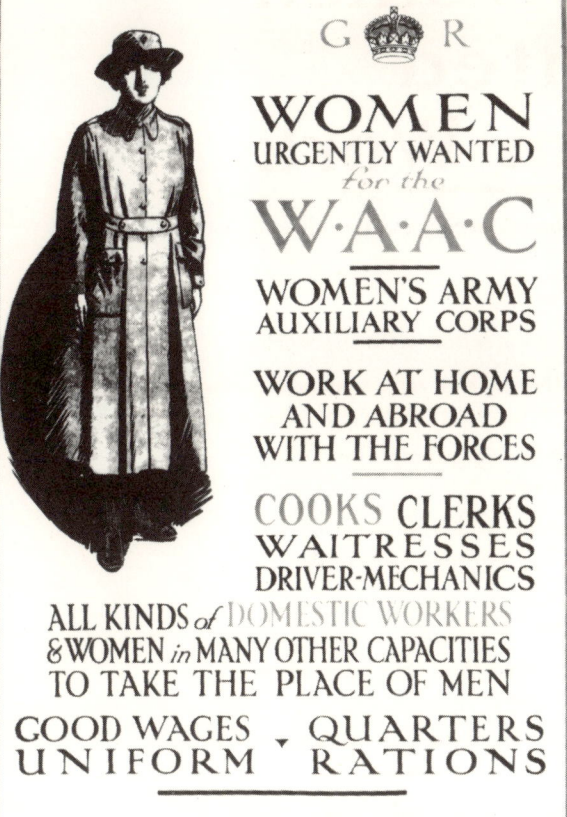

controllers and administrators, who could earn up to £500 per year (though few got more than £250); forewomen (instead of NCOs), and the rank and file who received 24-45s (£1.20-£2.25) per week. The Corps was divided into three sections: Cookery, Mechanical, and Clerical and Miscellaneous. Virtually all the tasks undertaken by them were traditionally "women's" work.

At the same time as the WAAC was established, the Women's Land Army came into being, in order to fill the gaps in farming. The number of women at work on the land rose by 33,000, many of them working-class girls. The organizers of the Land Army (middle- and upper-class women) were constantly worried about the behaviour and attitude of the girls, and the Official Handbook contained the following advice:

You are doing a man's work and so you are dressed rather like a man, but remember just because you wear a smock and breeches you should take care to behave like a British girl who expects chivalry and respect from everyone she meets.

35   Recruitment poster for the Land Army.

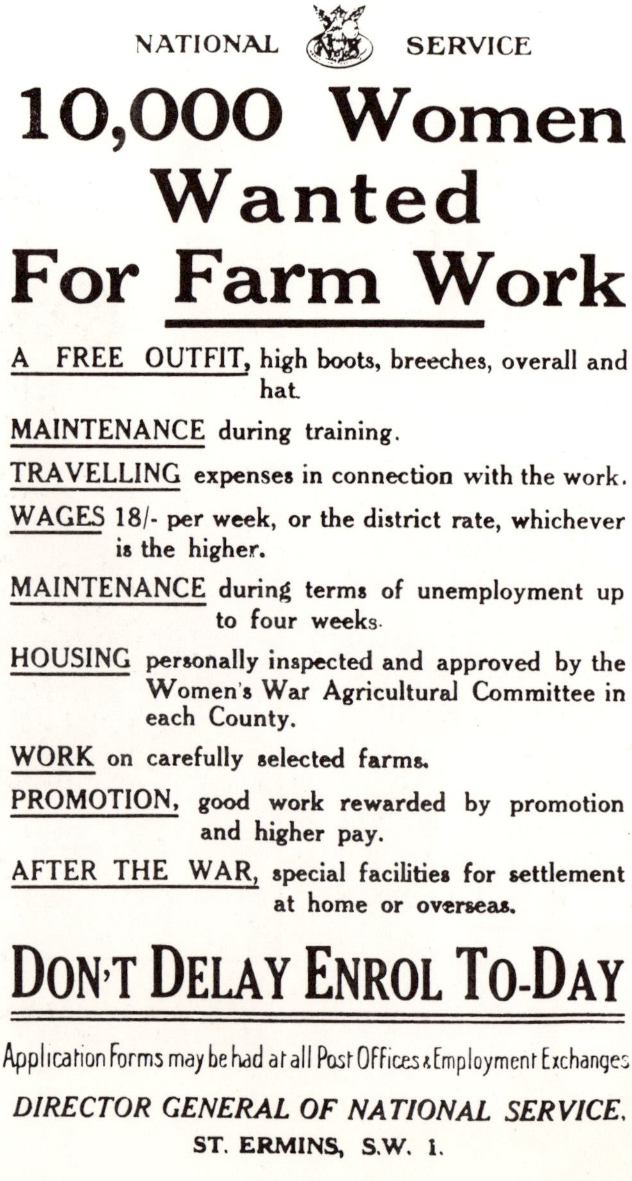

▼

NATIONAL 🦅 SERVICE

10,000 Women Wanted For Farm Work

A   FREE   OUTFIT, high boots, breeches, overall and hat.

MAINTENANCE during training.

TRAVELLING expenses in connection with the work.

WAGES 18/- per week, or the district rate, whichever is the higher.

MAINTENANCE during terms of unemployment up to four weeks.

HOUSING personally inspected and approved by the Women's War Agricultural Committee in each County.

WORK on carefully selected farms.

PROMOTION, good work rewarded by promotion and higher pay.

AFTER THE WAR, special facilities for settlement at home or overseas.

DON'T DELAY ENROL TO-DAY

Application Forms may be had at all Post Offices & Employment Exchanges.

DIRECTOR GENERAL OF NATIONAL SERVICE,
ST. ERMINS, S.W. 1.

But by the end of 1918 the sort of attitudes expressed in the handbook were becoming rather old-fashioned. Unintentionally, the war had brought about a change in women's attitudes to themselves. Even before the war women were beginning to be rather fed up with hearing that their place was at home. As Mary MacArthur put it:

They had begun to realise that those who talked of the home, really meant the kitchen.

Upper- and middle-class women now assumed that they had the right to work. Working-class women, doing "men's jobs", began to question the assumption that women were second-class workers. By the end of the war women were an established, if still small, section of the trade union movement.

The changes in attitude seemed to be affecting men as well as women. Between 1918 and 1920 *The Times* decided that women should be given the vote; a government enquiry accepted the justice of arguments for equal pay (though nothing was done about it); the government passed the Sex Disqualification Removal Act which gave women the right to enter the professions and enabled Oxford and Cambridge to award women degrees, though only Oxford acted upon it; and women over thirty were enfranchised on the same basis as men. It seemed possible that a real and permanent change in the status of women in society and at work was taking place.

36   Many women worked during the war at traditionally "female" tasks. Probably the largest group was the Voluntary Aid Detachment (VADs) who undertook unqualified nursing at the Front and at home.
▼

6
The Typewriter

The increase of clerical work

The war speeded up and confirmed changes which had begun to happen in women's employment long before August 1914. This was perhaps more true of women's employment in clerical and administrative jobs than anywhere else. In the four years of the war the number of women employed in clerical work in private firms in industry, banking and insurance increased by 500,000, while

the number doing the same sort of work for the government went up by 200,000. Some of the women were employed to replace men who had gone to the Front, but the vast majority of them were employed in new jobs. These jobs were partly created by the demands of the war, but, in private industry in particular, they were largely new jobs that would have been created anyway.

In an industrial society, once the factories have grown up and the making of goods is well under way, other sorts of jobs need to be done, in order to service the industries and make sure that they can run properly. As the factories grow, more people are needed to organize the buying of raw materials and the selling of the finished goods, and to organize paying the workers. Banks and insurance companies grow in size, in order to cope with new demands on them, and therefore they too need more office workers. As a result, in an *advanced industrial society*, the number of jobs for non-manual workers increases more quickly than for manual workers.

The people to fill these new jobs were found among those who had benefitted from the improved education available to the mass of people after 1870, and particularly among women — both middle- and working-class — who provided a pool of cheap labour. Between 1861 and 1911 the total working population of Britain increased by 77 per cent in men and 44.2 per cent in women. But in the growing non-manual jobs (teachers, shop assistants, clerks, and civil servants) men employed went up by 192.3 per cent and women by 307.0 per cent. In 1871 there were only 100,000 clerks employed in offices and banks, one third the number of coal miners. By 1911 there were over 500,000, whereas the number of coal miners remained roughly unchanged.

◄ 37   Women working in offices was seen by some as a threat. Society's idea of women is clearly portrayed in this cartoon from the turn of the century.

Shorthand and typing

Besides the need to employ people to cope with the new demands of office work, writing letters, keeping accounts, filing and recording, there was also a great need for increased speed and accuracy in completing these tasks. Two major developments in the late nineteenth century revolutionized office work and turned it from a task to which young men were apprenticed for a number of years into a task for which only a little training was necessary and which was thus "suitable" for women.

The first development was the growth of the use of shorthand. Shorthand had been used since very ancient times for such things as recording government business, but there did not seem much need for its wider application. However, in the mid-nineteenth century Isaac Pitman developed a new shorthand system, using signs for sounds. With all the enthusiasm of a missionary, he set about promoting his new shorthand which he saw as replacing writing everywhere. Great interest was shown in the idea by businessmen, and it was possibly first used in a systematic way in 1853 by the clerks in the Manchester, Sheffield & Lincolnshire Railway Offices. The innovation soon spread and people began to realize that shorthand "was to writing what the jenny was to the loom and the train to the coach". By the end of the century there was a shorthand clerk in every office.

The second innovation was the invention of the typewriter. Although a number of "perfect writing" machines had been made, it was not until 1868 that one appeared which was quicker than writing by hand. It was invented by an American printer and publisher called Christopher K. Sholes and he called it a typewriter — a word that came to be used both for the machine and for the person operating it. It was first made in the United Kingdom by Remington & Sons in 1873, and by 1882 typewriters were being bought in large numbers.

Other machines soon followed — calculating machines, addressing machines, duplicating machines, machines for sorting, stamping and sealing envelopes. Office workers developed different skills, so that different people carried out different tasks. The large majority were women and the most sought-after was the competent shorthand-typist.

Women clerical workers

With the development of office machines, the idea grew up that women were better than men at doing all the jobs in the office that now had to be undertaken. Some people suggested that, because the typewriter had keys like a piano, it was a machine suited to women! Others said that women could cope better than men with the repetitive routines and dead-end jobs which existed in the offices. It was thought that a woman's proper ambition was to get married, not to seek promotion in her job, and in the large majority of offices a marriage bar existed — women were expected to leave when they married. In the Civil Service this bar had the force of law.

39 and **40**   Before and After the Office Revolution. (Top) The General Office in Cadbury's in 1912, showing the male clerks at work, writing by hand. (Bottom) The Statistics Branch of the Ministry of Labour, after 1940. All the workers are women and all are using typewriters.

38   An early Remington typewriter.

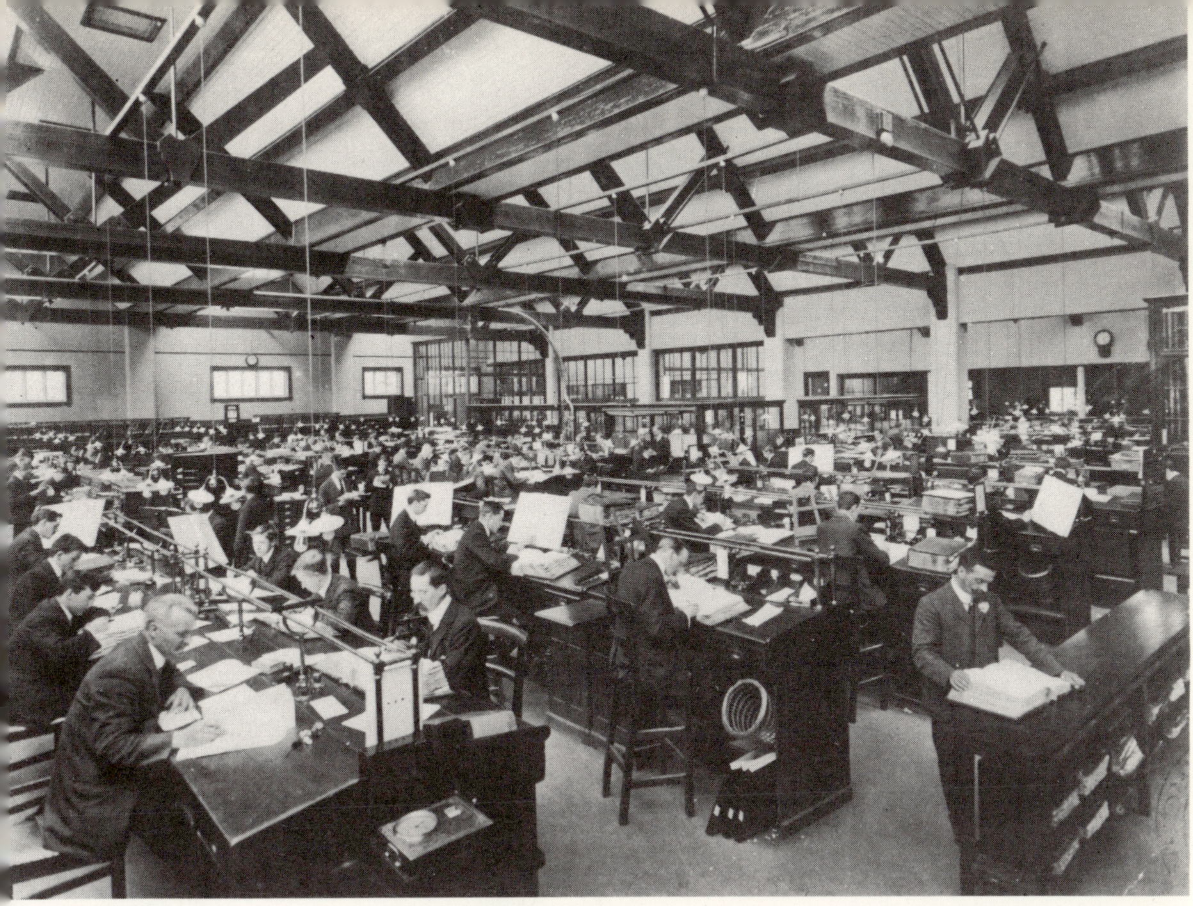

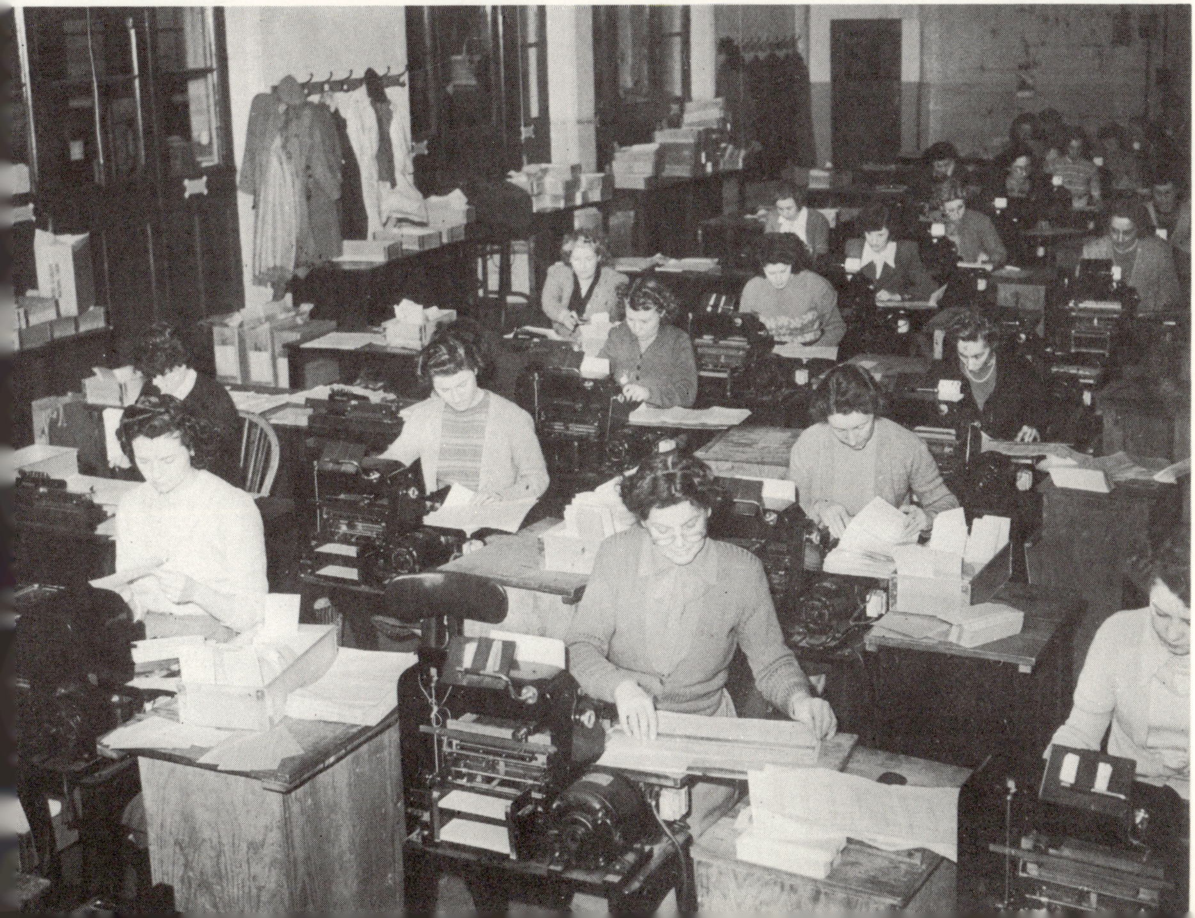

But the real reason why women were preferred to men was, once again, that they were a cheaper source of labour — a fact summed up neatly in an exchange between George Lansbury (a leading Socialist) and a clergyman giving evidence to the Royal Commission on the Poor Laws:

Lansbury: With regard to women, did I understand you that the employers tell you they are better adapted for the work of clerks and that sort of thing?
Witness: I said that a great many employers I had consulted frankly said that they preferred them.
Lansbury: And they paid them better wages than the men, I suppose?
Witness: I should not say that.
Lansbury: You would rather think, if they were so much more valuable that they would be paid better wages?
Witness: I do not think that follows at all.
Lansbury: Then it follows that a woman can give so much better value to the employer than a man and she gets less wages?
Witness: Yes, I suppose that is . . . the only conclusion you can draw.
Lansbury: Therefore the bottom fact of it is that the woman works cheaper?
Witness: Yes, decidedly.

In 1909-10 the inequalities in pay were marked. 54 per cent of the men employed in clerking jobs earned more than £100 a year, compared with 3 per cent of women; 46 per cent of men earned less than £100 a year compared with 97 per cent of women (and the vast majority of these women earned less than £50 a year).

There were three classes of women clerical workers. At the top were the women skilled in shorthand and typing and other office skills, who acted as secretaries. They earned between £2 and £4 a week. Then there were the copy typists, paid between £1 and £1.10s (£1.50) a week, and finally the general office worker whose pay was 10 to 15s (50 to 75p)

a week. They all began work at 9.00 a.m. — several hours later than women employed in industry and domestic service, and this was one of the main attractions of the job. They worked until 5.00 or 6.00 p.m.; overtime was not usually required and those who did it were rarely paid for it. Since clerking had the status of *contract labour* (that is, you were under contract for a year at a time), women clerks were entitled to paid holidays, which were a valuable perk. However, the conditions under which they worked — the level of heat and light in the offices, provision of toilet facilities and canteens, etc — were not controlled, and varied enormously from work place to work place, depending on the attitudes of the employers.

The quality of life which a woman clerk could attain was undoubtedly superior to that of women employed in industry. We can gather this from looking at the annual account of expenditure of an invoice typist of 1910, who worked in London and lived with her parents:

Income	£.	s.	d.
Wages (25s per week)	65.	0.	0.
Overtime		3.	0.
Xmas box from firm	1.	10.	0.
Present		5.	0.
	£66.	18.	0.

Expenditure	£.	s.	d.
Board and lodging	26.	0.	0.
Extra food (lunch & tea)	17.	2.	9.
Fares	8.	6.	9.
Dress	5.	9.	2.
Medicine		3.	2½.
Holidays and picnics	2.	15.	4½.
Amusement	2.	18.	4½.
Education (piano lessons)	1.	11.	1.
Books and papers		15.	2½.
Stamps and stationery		14.	10½.
Presents and collections	1.	16.	6.
Insurance		—	
Miscellaneous		17.	8½.
	£68.	11.	0.

Her expenditure on holidays and amusements is explained as follows:

Full wages were paid during the fortnight's holiday. The expenses on this holiday included 18s. for return fare and cab, £2.10s. for board and lodging for two weeks, 20s. 2d. for pleasure trips etc. and 2s. for tips.

The expenditure on amusements included the cost of tickets for a companion at the theatre, as well as on programmes, picture gallery catalogues and fares to and from the place of amusement. Thus theatres account for 29s.10d. for eight visits; concerts for 4s.4d. but in five cases out of eight no expense was incurred except for the programmes. Rinking [roller skating] including fares and admission accounted for 10s.4½d. records for a 'talking machine' cost 9s.8d.

Clerking was considered a very respectable occupation, far too respectable for those employed in it to seek trade union membership — and, as a result, there was even more difficulty in organizing trade unions among clerks than among women in general. There were other difficulties as well, such as the very high turnover among the people who worked as clerks and the great difficulty of bringing together people scattered in small and very small work places.

Nevertheless, the National Union of Clerks was founded in 1897, though by 1900 it still had only eighty-two members. From the start, women held equal rights in the union with men, but even so, by 1914, women, though the majority of workers in offices, formed only 12 per cent of the union's membership. Despite these rather shaky beginnings, the National Union of Clerks grew into APEX (the Association of Professional, Executive and Clerical Workers), which is one of the most prominent unions in the TUC today.

Generally, the turnover of clerks was high, but, in spite of the routine nature of the work in the offices, some ambitious and hard-working women did secure promotion and rise from the position of general office worker to confidential secretary. The war helped speed up this process.

Madeline Veysey was the first woman to be employed in the office at Risca Colliery in South Wales. She had intended to be a teacher, but ill-health prevented her continuing at the local county school to which she had won a scholarship. In 1914, aged fourteen, she began work in a timber merchant's office in Newport, earning eight shillings (40p) a week, where she learnt to type by practice. She was employed at general office work and one of her main jobs was to copy letters into the letter-book. This letter-book was used for years, even though carbon paper existed. It was not until the 1920s that carbon copies became common. The Newport office had one other woman working there — the general secretary — who had learnt shorthand at a typing school in Newport.

The demand for office workers had led to the setting up of a number of private schools and colleges to teach commercial skills, and by 1900 a number of Local School Boards were running shorthand and typing courses in evening classes. It was to one of these that Madeline Veysey went to learn shorthand. She took a term's lessons for a very small fee and then had a term's private tuition, costing fifteen shillings (75p), from Mr Richards, who was second in charge of the office in the local steel works.

By now the war had broken out and local businesses were planning to take on women staff, as the men were liable to call-up. At the central office of Risca Colliery (in Crosskeys) they built separate cloakroom facilities first, and in March 1916 Madeline Veysey began work there. She was not quite

41   Women learning to receive and send telegraph messages in Morse Code at the Female School of Telegraphy, Moorgate Street.

sixteen. Being the first woman employed in the office, she had a great fuss made of her; boys rushed to open doors — but that wore off after a while.

At first, she was employed as the telephone operator on the switchboard at ten shillings (50p) a week, but before long she was promoted to filling in the pay books — a responsible job for which the pay was £1 per week — high for the area.

In 1917 the Commercial Agent's secretary was dismissed and Madeline Veysey was promoted to take her place. Her pay was now £2.10s. (£2.50) a week — more than a school teacher's. As a secretary, she had an office of her own, with her own desk and typewriter. Her official hours were nine to five, but she was expected to work as needed and a car would often be sent to her home in the evenings to bring her back to work. She got no overtime pay, but was occasionally given the odd day off. During the war she got ten days' holiday a year at the most, but the usual holiday allowance was a fortnight, with pay, and all Bank Holidays. Because Madeline Veysey's father was dead, she was regarded as the family's breadwinner, and got coal at the special low rate for colliers of

6s.6d. (32½p) per ton. All the office staff, including the women, got a goose at Christmas. At first, the girls had been expected to wear a black apron, but this was soon dropped and most of them wore a blouse and skirt or sometimes a dress.

When the war ended, some of the women in the office lost their jobs, but not those who had been taken on to deal with increased office work and who therefore had not replaced men. In the early 1920s compto-meters (machines that could add, subtract, multiply and divide) were added to the office equipment and two girls from Risca were sent on a training course — run by the firm that made them — to learn how to use them.

In 1925 Madeline Veysey was earning £5 a week — a very high wage in South Wales at the time. But in that year she left work — and married the Commercial Agent!

The future of office work

By 1925 office work of all descriptions was very much a woman's world and has re-mained so. Male secretaries are few and far between. But whereas the "office revolution" of the late nineteenth century led to a great expansion in female employment, the threatened "office revolution" of the late twentieth century, with the introduction of silicone chip processes, is expected to bring massive cut-backs in this area of women's work.

42   Miss Sue Dorsey at her office desk, February 1918.

▼

7
Depression and War

Post-war hopes

1919 appeared to be a year of great promise. The soldiers returning from France were promised a "land fit for heroes". The government had given women over the age of thirty the vote, and the Sex Disqualification Act was on the Statute Book. This act enabled women to become magistrates, serve on juries, enter the legal profession and upper ranks of the Civil Service, and removed all legal barriers to their membership of Oxford and Cambridge Universities.

The numbers of women in trade unions continued to rise. When women war workers returned to peacetime industry, such as working in laundries, they took their trade unionism with them. Membership of the NFWW had increased from 11,000 in 1914 to 60,000 in 1919.

A government committee in 1918 recommended equal pay, and women in the trade union movement were strong enough to press for this recommendation to be acted upon, as well as calling for a forty-eight-hour week and improved maternity leave for women at work. Their stand on equal pay, which was most strongly supported by professional women workers, such as teachers and civil servants, received official approval in the Treaty of Versailles, which ended the First World War, and among other things endorsed the principle of equal pay.

Women were now such an established part of the trade union movement that it no longer seemed appropriate for their organizations to be separate. The Women's Trade Union League was absorbed into the TUC and the National Federation of Women Workers merged with the General & Municipal Workers Union.

Hopes for the new post-war world were short-lived, however. Already in 1919 women were being discharged to make way for ex-servicemen. A government Committee on Women in Industry produced another report on equal pay, opposing the idea, and even the popular press were quick to forget women's work in the war. The *Daily Graphic* wrote:

The idea that because the State called for women to help the nation, the State must continue to employ them is too absurd for serious women to entertain.

In 1920 the economy began to collapse and by July 1921 there were over two million men and women unemployed. The years of the depression had begun and by 1930 unemployment was to reach three million.

43 A meeting of women trade unionists, ➤ organized by the TUC General Council during Congress Week at Bournemouth in 1926.

The depression

Throughout the depression women workers were both better and worse off than men. On the one hand, working-class women were finding employment opportunities in the light industries, making the newly invented consumer goods of the twentieth century, such as vacuum cleaners. These industries were less badly hit by the depression than the more established industries such as iron and steel making, coal mining and ship building. The one industry where working-class women were seriously affected was textiles, which was particularly badly affected both by increased competition from abroad and by new processes which speeded up the work and further reduced the numbers of jobs available.

Administration continued to expand and so the jobs of most office workers were safe. In one or two areas where women had replaced men during the war, they remained in employment (e.g. the grocery and provisions trade). In the professions, too,

44 and **45**   A pair of Labour party posters, issued in 1923 for the general election of that year. For many working people, the economic hardships of the years following the war seemed a poor reward for the efforts made from 1914-18.

you were unlikely to lose your job if you had one — unless of course you got married, for the marriage bars were strengthened and extended until almost every employer could dismiss a woman worker on marriage.

▼

YESTERDAY - THE TRENCHES

PUBLISHED BY THE LABOUR PARTY, 33 Eccleston Square, London, S.W. & printed by VINCENT BROOKS DAY & SON LTD, 48 Parker St, Kingsway, London W1

On the other hand, one of the great difficulties for many women, as well as men, was finding a job in the first place. There was a possible way out for women in that they could enter domestic service (an extra 200,000 women became servants between 1921 and 1931); but for many this was a horrifying necessity, as domestic servants had very little freedom and were closely supervised. The way, too, in which women

TO-DAY–UNEMPLOYED

PUBLISHED BY THE LABOUR PARTY 33 Eccleston Square London S.W. & PRINTED BY VINCENT BROOKS DAY & SON LTD 48 Parker St. Kingsway London WC2

46   Job-hunting in the 1930s.

were forced into this work caused much resentment, and was a consequence of the manner in which benefits to the unemployed were administered in the inter-war years.

It was in this area that women were much worse off than men. In 1920 the National Insurance scheme, which had been started by the Liberal government in 1911 and through which workers were insured against unemployment and sickness, was extended to cover almost all workers, except domestic servants, agricultural workers and one or two other groups. The increase in unemployment was thought to be temporary, and the benefits available to unemployed workers would help cushion the change from war conditions to a peacetime economy. Insured workers claiming benefit could receive extra

allowances for dependants. Women, however, received less benefit than men, although their contributions while in work were the same.

But it soon became clear that unemployment was not a temporary thing, and before long more money was being drawn out in benefits than had been paid in in contributions. The rest of the '20s and '30s saw a series of governments determined to cut back on benefits and make the books balance. All unemployed workers suffered from this policy and women more than most.

Benefit could only be paid to those "genuinely seeking work". Since there was a high demand for domestic workers, any woman refusing to take such a job — regardless of her qualifications — would have her benefit stopped on the grounds that she was not genuinely seeking work. If she took such a job and subsequently lost it, she lost all rights to benefit, for domestic service was *not* included in the insurance scheme. If she expressed a willingness to do domestic work, but could not find any, she could also be excluded as she was "unlikely to *be* employed in insurable work".

In 1931 the National Government introduced the Anomalies Regulations in a further attempt to cut the cost of unemployment benefit. These hit particularly hard at married women. Within a month 134,000 had had their right to benefit disallowed. The introduction of the Means Test in November 1931 affected huge numbers of unemployed. Any wages of anyone living in your home or any hard-earned savings meant a reduction in benefit.

In 1936 a survey into poverty in York

estimated that a weekly wage of thirty-one shillings (£1.55) was necessary for a single woman to live above the poverty line. The benefit payable to the few who qualified was fifteen shillings (75p) a week.

One of the tragic consequences of the depression and the discrimination against working women was the enormous rise in the number of babies who died at birth. Many women were afraid to leave work for a minute, knowing that they would never get the job back. Some babies were born in the factories. Other women, who could find a sympathetic doctor, took a day off with "lumbago" and were back at their work benches often within hours of the birth. It was hardly surprising that many of these babies died, but the possession of a job, however badly paid, was the key to the whole family's survival.

During the early 1930s the National Unemployed Workers Movement organized

47 A mass demonstration of unemployed men and women in Hyde Park, London, October, 1932.

▼

great hunger marches from the areas most affected by the depression to London, to demand an end to the Means Test and more jobs. In 1932 and 1934 the marches included women's contingents from all the large industrial towns of the north, where the collapse of the textile industry had hit women particularly badly. (In 1938 the amount of cloth exported from Britain was the lowest since 1851.) In 1934 the women, led by Maud Brown, sent a deputation to Downing Street where they were seen by Ishbel MacDonald, the Prime Minister's daughter. They tried in vain to point out to her that domestic service was not an alternative for women skilled in their own trades.

The Second World War

As the thirties drew to a close, the problem of unemployment began to be eased as industries were expanded to cope with rearmament, in response to the threatening situation developing in Europe. The Second World War, which broke out on 3 September 1939, heralded the return to work of thousands of women needed to "help the nation" as they had been in the First World War.

During the first months of the war, as in 1914, large numbers of women became unemployed as the demand for peacetime goods fell. Other women, still employed in metal and engineering trades, were working an eighty- or ninety-hour week to provide war materials. It was 1941 before formal organization of labour in the war began.

A Manpower Requirements Committee was set up to estimate the needs of war industries and the armed services. They decided that one and a half million women would be needed over and above the five million already in the workforce in 1939.

48　The end of unemployment came with the start of war, and by 1943 any woman aged between eighteen and fifty might be conscripted. The Auxiliary Territorial Service (ATS) in the north of England. (The ATS later became the WRAC.)
▼

In March 1941 all women were required to register at a labour exchange and in December 1941 the National Service No.2 Act was passed, which conscripted single women between the ages of twenty and thirty into the armed forces, auxiliary services (such as anti-aircraft batteries) and industry. By the end of 1943 all women between eighteen and fifty could be conscripted where there was no compelling domestic reason against their working.

The recognized need for women workers still did not bring equality, either from the government or from the leadership of the TUC. While the General Council did succeed

49 Women at work in the aircraft construction industry during the Second World War.

▼

in getting equal compensation for women with men in war injuries, on the grounds that:

Woman's life is at least as valuable as a man's and her physical and mental well-being are just as important . . . ,

they accepted without complaint that injured women and girls should receive lower wages than men and boys at government re-training centres.

The persistent problem faced by women workers of organizing both home and work was recognized by the government and a number of measures were taken to ease the double burden. State-run nurseries were widely established, and a system of shared jobs developed — where two women did one job — so that domestic responsibilities could be met. Factory welfare provision was widely extended and, for the first time, the plea of the Dundee jute workers, made almost one hundred years before, for a place to hang their coats, was met and this became the right of every woman worker.

Trade union membership increased significantly and the Amalgamated Engineers Union at last admitted women to membership. In 1943 the trade union movement accepted that women wage earners had an equal right to employment with men and that sex should not be a basis for determining wage rates.

When the war ended in 1945, women workers were in an even more powerful position than they had been in 1918. It might now prove possible to win equal pay and equal opportunities with men in all fields of employment.

50 Excellent free state nurseries were widely established during the war. Britain now has less than half the number of nurseries that existed in 1942, thus compounding the difficulties that many working women face today.

▼

8
Towards Equality

Equal pay

In the twenty years following the end of the Second World War women workers won one major victory. This was the achievement of equal pay for professional workers in the civil service and in teaching.

In 1944 Parliament passed a major Education Act which raised the school leaving age to fifteen and led to the introduction of the eleven plus examination.

51 A secondary modern school in the 1950s. The principle of equal pay for women teachers was won in 1955, but the average woman teacher still earns less than her average male colleague.

Another clause in the act made it illegal to dismiss a woman teacher from employment when she married. During discussion of the bill a Conservative MP, Mrs Cazelet-Keir, had moved an amendment to ensure that men and women teachers got the same pay. The amendment was passed at this stage, but the government decided to make the issue one of confidence and, when the equal pay question was put to the whole House, it was defeated. However, it was impossible to ignore the demands being made by women teachers and civil servants, and so the government set up a Royal Commission to look at the whole question of equal pay for women.

The Commission reported in October 1946. It completely rejected the idea of equal pay in industrial work. And, while it recognized that men and women teachers did such similar work that it was one and the same, it nevertheless rejected the case for equal pay in this area too. One of the arguments used was that men would be discouraged from entering teaching if equal pay were awarded. Another was that women had always been willing to work for less. The Commission also accepted the argument that men had families to support and there-fore deserved more, conveniently ignoring that no distinctions were made against single men or in favour of women who were the "breadwinners" in their families.

In effect, the Commission endorsed the findings of the government enquiries held at the end of the First World War. But times had changed. Support for equal pay was much more widespread than it had been twenty-five years before. Women teachers and civil servants were much more organized and determined and mounted a campaign which included a documentary film about equal pay, which was seen at cinemas as well as at private showings, a huge demon-stration in Trafalgar Square in 1951 demanding "Equal Pay for Equal Work Now", and a large petition which was eventually delivered to the government in 1954.

On its own, this would not have been enough, but the immediate post-war years saw a marked rise in the birth rate which, in its turn, led to a shortage of teachers. The economic arguments against equal pay were undermined. More teachers had to be found; married women teachers in particular had to be attracted back to the profession. In 1955 the government awarded civil servants and teachers equal pay, to be gradually introduced over the next seven years. In October 1955 the Equal Pay Campaign Committee held a "Milestone Dinner" to celebrate the victory.

This was a victory for only some women workers, however. The vast majority of women were untouched by this equal pay victory. In 1963 the TUC adopted its first Charter for Women, which outlined a series of demands which would give women equality as workers for the first time. It called for equal pay for work of equal value; improved opportunities for promotion and training; more apprenticeship schemes for girls and better re-training facilities for older women; and improved health and welfare provisions for women workers. The govern-ment resisted all these demands, and the sixties saw a widening of the gaps in pay between men and women as pay freeze succeeded pay freeze.

Then, in 1968, a group of women machin-ists at Fords in Dagenham took up the demand for equal pay, forced their union to support the strike and, with a lot of public support, gained the regrading they were looking for. Their stand brought an immediate response from women workers in the trade union movement and from other women. At the Trades Union Congress of 1968 a resolution was passed which advocated the use of industrial action to press for equal pay for women. A group of Labour MPs introduced an Equal Pay Bill, and Joyce Butler, a woman MP, put forward an Anti-

52 Civil servants campaigning for equal pay in ►
1954. For them, too, the principle was conceded in 1955.

62

RIGHTS
DISCRIMINATION
PAY
RIGHTS
IN

EQUAL PAY
GENERAL & MUNICIPAL WORKERS
THE AIM OF THE GENERAL & MUNICIPAL WORKE
LH 101

Discrimination Bill which aimed at ending
all discrimination against women — not just
discrimination in pay. A Campaign
Committee for Equal Women's Rights was
formed, which demanded an end to sex
discrimination and the adoption of equal
legal rights for women.

In 1970 the government submitted to
pressure and introduced an Equal Pay Act.
This allowed firms five years in which to
ensure that women doing "like work", or
work graded as being similar to a man's,
received equal pay. This was a narrow
definition of equal pay. The Common Market
countries had adopted a policy of equal pay
for work of equal value, which could be used
to cover women in every sort of job. The
British law effectively excluded women
working in predominantly female occupations. Even so, many women did benefit
and the difference between men's and
women's wages in the 1970s began to
narrow. However, equal pay is still a long
way from being achieved. In 1970, for
example, women's hourly rate of pay as a
percentage of men's was 63 per cent. By
1977 this had increased, but only to 75.5 per
cent, and 1978 saw a decline to 74 per cent.

Equal rights

Throughout the 1970s women, both inside
and outside the trade union movement,
continued to campaign for equal rights.
Equal pay was only a small part of the
battle. Women still faced discrimination

at work, in both training and job opportunities. They still had little help and support
in combining the dual responsibilities of
home and work and still faced more legal
restrictions than men.

1975 was designated International
Women's Year by the United Nations and
in that year a series of acts were passed by
Parliament which began to outlaw discrimination against women in a number of
fields. The Sex Discrimination Act made it
illegal to discriminate against women in jobs,
services, housing and education, and set up
the Equal Opportunities Commission to
monitor the law and promote equality. The
Employment Protection Act guaranteed
maternity leave and maternity pay for
women who had worked for the same
employer for more than two years, and the
Social Security Pensions Act extended the
numbers of women entitled to a full pension
and made it illegal to discriminate against
women in pension schemes — provided they
were doing the same sort of work as men.

But, as the chain makers in Birmingham
had discovered seventy years before, legislation does not guarantee equality. A report
of the Manpower Services Commission — a
government body — published in 1979,
concluded that although equality of opportunity might be protected by legislation, it
was not yet a reality. The proportion of
unemployed women had doubled between
1973 and 1978 and stood at 29.4 per cent.
This was a result of the decline in job
opportunities in the areas in which the large
majority of women were still employed —
clerical work, education, welfare and health,
and selling. The areas where shortages of
skilled workers existed, such as mechanical
engineering and the chemical industry, were
not traditional employers of women and
were reluctant to employ women at all.

Many employers preferred men because
they had always held such jobs, and they
used recruitment methods which discouraged
girls from applying. They were not convinced
that women were as suitable, because of

55 "We're never satisfied" – the Women's Liberation Movement's Sex Discrimination Campaign demonstrate outside the House of Commons, June 1975. The Sex Discrimination Act could not guarantee equality, in fact. Laws do not immediately change society's attitudes.

◄ 56 An engineer at work.

57 (Right, top) 1976: the first woman ► auctioneer at Sotheby's, Miss Libby Howie, aged twenty-four.

58 In 1972, for the first time in Britain, women ► jockeys competed in a horse race at Kempton Park.

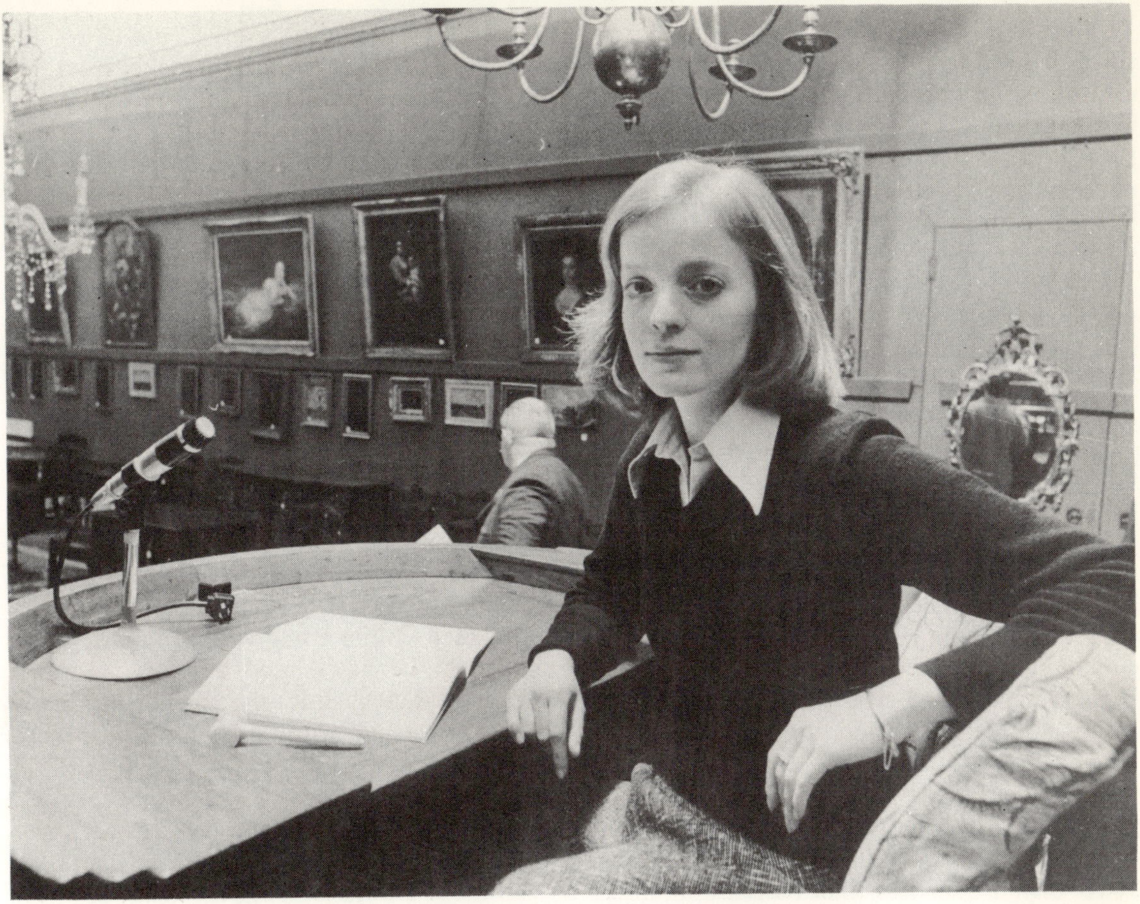

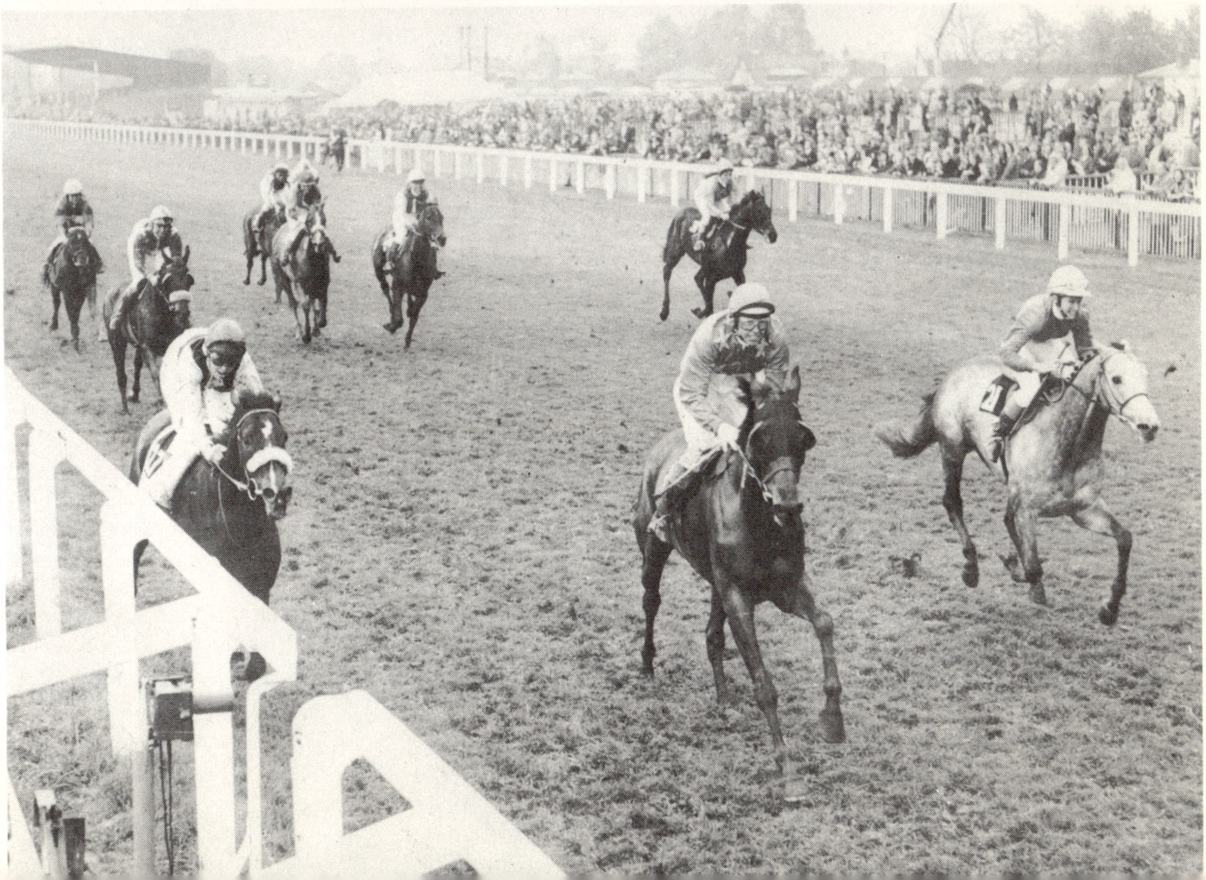

their belief in differences in intelligence, aptitude and strength between men and women. And, though many employers thought women more hardworking and conscientious than men, they also believed that the turnover and absenteeism among women employees were higher.

The Manpower Commission's report as a whole revealed very clearly that a change in law does not necessarily result in a change in attitude and that women who wish to achieve success at work still need to be as determined as Gertrude Bell was when she set out to chart areas of Arabia unknown to westerners.

Another area where little change has taken place in a hundred years is among the 750,000 women still engaged in out-work. A report from the Low Pay Unit in 1975 concluded that pay and conditions for these women were little better than those exposed by Mary MacArthur and the Anti-Sweating League in 1906. For many of these women there is no alternative source of employment, as their family responsibilities prevent them from seeking work outside the home. In 1970 Britain had less than half the number of nurseries provided in 1942. Only 4 per cent of three- and four-year-olds could go to nursery schools, compared to one third in 1908 and compared to over 50 per cent in other Common Market countries. In 1979 the government proposed a further cut in the provision of pre-school education and nurseries.

In the hundred or so years covered by this book great changes have taken place in the world of women's work. Both middle-class and working-class women form a major part of our workforce, with almost ten million women in employment. Almost half of them are now in trade unions. Equal pay is on the Statute Book and established in the professions. It is theoretically illegal to discriminate against a woman on the grounds of her sex and, apart from certain safeguards to do with health and safety, any job is open to her.

But women architects, jockeys, stock-brokers, carpenters are still the exception. Society's attitudes still make it difficult for women to take up a full and satisfying place in the world of work. Women still earn significantly less than men and are not fairly represented among the higher ranks of the workforce. The idea of the wage for the family man remains dominant, as does the conviction that a woman's paid work is incidental to her "real" function of home-maker. Economic realities that require a woman to work (both the family who needs her wage and society which needs her labour) are ignored, as are the desire and right of many women to have more to occupy their lives than the daily grind of housework and dirty nappies.

If Mary Collier could visit Britain in 1980, she might be bewildered by cars, television and aeroplanes, but she would probably instantly recognize the difficulties still faced by women at work:

> When Ev'ning does approach we
> homeward hie
> And our Domestic Toils incessant ply . . .
> Our Toil and Labour's daily so extreme
> That we have hardly ever Time to dream.

A cable splicer, USA. ▶

Some
Key Dates

1850   First Girls' Public Day School founded

1854   First Girls' Public Boarding School founded

1868   Typewriter invented

1869   Girton College, Cambridge, founded

1874   Women's Trade Union League founded

1875   First women attend the Trades Union Congress

1879   Lady Margaret Hall, Oxford, founded

1888   Match Girls' Strike

1893   First woman factory inspector appointed

1906   National Federation of Women Workers founded

1910   Trade Boards Act: wages boards set up to establish minimum wages in some industries

       Chain Makers Strike

1914-1918   First World War

1915   National Registration Scheme: women as well as men required to register

1917   WAAC and WRNS founded

       Women's Land Army started

1918   Women over thirty win the right to vote

1919   Sex Disqualification Act: legal barriers removed on women entering some of the professions

1939-1945   Second World War

1941   National Service No.2 Act: single women conscripted into the armed services and other war industries

1955   Women teachers and civil servants win equal pay

1963   The first Women's Charter adopted by the TUC

1970   Equal Pay Act

1975   Sex Discrimination Act : discrimination against women made illegal in certain areas

       Employment Protection Act: maternity leave and maternity pay guaranteed in certain circumstances

Books for Further Reading

John Burnett (Ed),
Useful Toil,
Autobiographies of Working People from the
1820s to 1920s, Allen Lane, 1974

Ross Davies,
Women and Work,
Hutchinson, 1975

Richard Gray,
Working Lives
(Vol 1 1905-45), Hackney W.E.A. with
Centreprise Publishing Project

Lee Holcombe,
Victorian Ladies at Work,
David & Charles, 1973

Jill Kiddington and Jill Norris,
One Hand Tied Behind Us,
Virago, 1978

Sheila Lewenhak,
Women and Trade Unions,
Ernest Benn, 1977

Lindsay Mackie & Polly Pattullo,
Women at Work,
Tavistock, 1977

Arthur Marwick,
Women at War, 1914 — 1918,
Croom Helm, 1977

Sheila Rowbotham,
Hidden from History, 300 Years of Women's
Oppression and the Fight Against It,
Pluto Press, 1973

Index

The numbers in **bold type** refer to the figure numbers of the illustrations